CLASSIC
BUS

YEARBOOK – 7

Edited by Gavin Booth

Ian Allan
PUBLISHING

CONTENTS

First published 2001

ISBN 0 7110 2827 3

Design by Hieroglyph

Published by Ian Allan Publishing

An imprint of Ian Allan Publishing Ltd, Hersham, Surrey KT12 4RG

Printed by Ian Allan Printing Ltd, Hersham, Surrey KT12 4RG

Code: 0104/B2

INTRODUCTION

WE ALWAYS aim for variety in *Classic Bus Yearbook*, and this seventh edition includes articles and photo-features covering a wide variety of topics, written and contributed by a range of writers and photographers, many of them new to these pages – but with a fair selection of popular and familiar names.

Paul Watts has written a memory of Southdown's Moulsecoomb garage, and we know from correspondence received at *Classic Bus* magazine that Southdown was one of the most popular bus fleets in the country. Another new name is John S Hinchliffe, who looks back at bus services in the 'Summer Wine' country of Yorkshire's Holme Valley. David Beilby describes Todmorden's Indian Summer, when the JOC buses held on to their individuality before being absorbed into the Calderdale undertaking.

G E Hawkyard covers the history of the Middlesex-based coachbuilder, Whitson, still fondly remembered for its innovative and stylish bodies.

David Wayman is a regular CB contributor, and he provides a portrait of Sunderland's Park Lane bus station in the 1950s. Michael Dryhurst returns to a popular topic – the fitting of four-bay and five-bay bodies on postwar double-deckers.

Robert E Jowitt's distinctive prose and photographic styles turn to Hants & Dorset's route 47 between Winchester and Southampton – and there's the inevitable romantic interest to record.

Our London offering is Chris Drew's story of Green Line's double-deckers over the years, illustrated with Chris's splendid line drawings.

Tony Moyes recalls how he discovered the village of Maenclochog in the 1970s, illustrated with his distinctive rural photos.

Portugal has long been popular with UK enthusiasts looking for British-built buses, and although their numbers are falling fast, we recall the heady days when AECs, Daimlers and Leylands were commonplace in that lovely country.

Photographic essays include C B Golding on a day trip to Bradford in 1963, seeking out trolleybuses, and Geoff Mills on the variety that could be found in Sudbury in the 1960s.

Two colour Portfolio features illustrate the work of Robin Hannay, on odd secondhand purchases, and Iain MacGregor on Edinburgh Corporation buses.

Regular features from *Classic Bus* magazine are Checkpoint, where Alan Millar provides a potted history on a variety of topics, and Roger and Out, where Roger Davies looks back from a busman's point-of-view. And, in his variation on the regular magazine feature Classic Blunderbus, Alan Millar offers another Classic Wonderbus, this time the Leyland Titan PD2.

Classic Bus magazine is published every two months and includes a mix of articles rather like this Yearbook. The magazine's strapline is 'Remembering buses the way they used to be'. We hope this book helps you to do that – and if you haven't started taking the magazine yet, you'll find it in good newsagents and bookstalls.

Gavin Booth
Edinburgh

Front cover: *The activities of preservationists keep the memory of classic buses alive. This fine 1955 Bristol KSW6B with 55-seat ECW body, new to Thames Valley, is typical of many buses delivered to Tilling Group companies in the 1950s.*
John Robinson

Page 1: *At one time it looked as if double-deckers would dominate London Transport's Green Line network of express coach services. Chris Drew looks at Green Line double-deckers on pages 68-75, illustrated with his line drawings like this view of Routemaster RMC1456.*

Back cover, upper: *A less familiar Bristol/ECW product was the little SUL4A with underfloor-mounted Albion engine, designed for rural operations. This preserved 1961 example with 33-seat dual-purpose body, was new to Western National.*
John Robinson

Back cover, lower: *The London Transport RF type, voted by Classic Bus readers as the Classic Single-Deck Bus of the Century, went into service 50 years ago, and this anniversary is being marked by various events in 2001. NLE 633 of 1953, in Country Area green, is one of well over 100 RFs preserved.*
John Robinson

THE MOULSE

PAUL WATTS remembers a Southdown garage

The author's five minutes of fame as he prepares to drive the last bus from Eastbourne Bus Station on 8 August 1980 at 22.30hrs. The bus is of course a Southdown Leyland National.

WASN'T IT Andy Warhol who said that everyone has 15 minutes of fame? My own 15 minutes of fame was actually just five minutes when, at 22.30hrs on Saturday 8 September 1980, I was recorded by BBC local radio prior to driving the last bus ever out of Southdown's bus station at Eastbourne. No great shakes, I guess, in the big post-modern media circus in which we all now live. I do remember though, being a tad saddened by the passing of another piece of British transport history. Correspondents to *Classic Bus* have lamented that old bus stations and garages are being torn down or transformed into retail space, and likewise I have unhappily to report that in Eastbourne the bus station is now a pair of uninspiring shops.

Southdown in the early 1980s, like other operators around the country, was starting what was euphemistically referred to as rationalisation. In truth this often meant asset-stripping and the selling of prime-site real estate; quite soon many bus stations, garages and dormies started to disappear. All of the company's property became fair game. I was based at one such location: a small town garage on the outskirts of Brighton in an area called Moulsecoomb. Thankfully not reduced to the ignominy of supermarket redevelopment – like so many – Moulsecoomb garage survives relatively unscathed and currently houses some milk floats and refrigeration equipment of South Coast Dairies. It is still remembered with immense fondness by the crews that worked there, and many I spoke to associate it with the 'golden years' of Southdown.

OOMB STORY

Beginnings

The garage at Moulsecoomb was built during late 1956 and it opened for operation in the summer or 1957. Paul Williams, now operations manager at Brighton & Hove Buses, used to work for Southdown: 'I was traffic superintendent in Brighton in the early 1970s and Moulsecoomb was one of my depots. I was responsible for Edward Street, Freshfield Road, Moulsecoomb and Lewes, and also outstations at Hassocks and Henfield.' Did Paul know anything of the history of Moulsecoomb Garage?

'Southdown was unique in having their own architect in those days, they did all their own designing and had a clerk of works. Moulsecoomb Garage was designed by H A F Spooner. Outside contractors, I think, did the actual building.'

Just recently, I was fortunate enough to meet again one man who has, more than anyone else, been embroidered into the history of that place. He is my old boss: Leading Driver (later Garage Inspector) Mickey Webb. In charge of the garage for fifteen years between 1969 and 1984, Mickey is a fount of much 'Moulsecoombular' knowledge. He seems to think that along with the above mentioned contractors were also many Southdown staff.

'It was built by Southdown itself', he said, 'and a lot of labour was provided by the tour drivers, who

had to find something to do during the winter months. They usually stood 'spare' in Edward Street when there wasn't a lot of coaching work to do. So Southdown sent them to Moulsecoomb, painting and labouring during that winter. I remember one guy, Driver Paine was his name, once telling me that he'd been up there painting girders etc balancing on top of an old tallboy!'

Health and safety issues aside, the garage opened and as reported in 'The Southdown Story 1915-1965': '. . accommodation for vehicles at Brighton, which had been eased by extensive alterations to the Freshfield Road depot, was further increased by the construction of the new garage at Moulsecoomb.' Indeed, some 30 double-deck buses were billeted there.

'Billet' seems to be the most appropriate word, for as Paul Williams recalls: 'Although it had pits – to the best of my memory – it wasn't used as an engineering base. I think a fitter may have called first thing in the morning to change light bulbs and any minor works going on, but generally speaking it was just used as a parking garage.'

A handsome beast by any standards – Southdown Leyland PD2/12 no.768 (OCD 768) with Park Royal 57-seat body has just been fuelled and washed at Edward Street before being ferried to Moulsecoomb for overnight parking.

One of Southdown's legendary Queen Marys, no.838 (VUF 838) of Moulsecoomb garage, a Leyland Titan PD3/4 with Northern Counties 69-seat bodywork, en route from Lower Bevendean to Brighton.
Surfleet

Paul explained that although (in the late 1960s) some buses 'were allocated to the garage and some drivers and conductors would book on there and take buses out, at most times the buses were actually ferried backwards and forwards to Edward Street and were used by Edward Street men'. He continues: 'Edward Street was somewhat restricted in size and there wasn't enough parking space. I can remember in the evenings a driver at Edward Street would bring a bus in and book it off; it would then be fuelled and washed and a shunting driver would run it 'light' to Moulsecoomb and park it. This was pre-National Bus Company.' However, Moulsecoomb became much more that just a 'parking' garage and in time took on a life of its own.

Mickey's Moulsecoomb

It would be helpful at this point to give some historical context. At the time that Moulsecoomb garage was built, Britain was just beginning to shake off the manacles of postwar austerity. Around Britain light industrial estates were burgeoning and contiguous with these the necessary living space for its workforce. When Mickey Webb took over the running of Moulsecoomb garage in 1969 large estates had already grown up in Coldean, Hollingbury,

Lower Bevendean and Moulsecoomb. The role of his garage had already started to grow. Did Mickey Webb think of Moulsecoomb as a parking overspill? 'No, no, it was a garage in its own right; it had its own specific routes'. He gives the following example: 'I used to run 13 contract buses to Allen West (the factory complex next door) when I first took the garage over. We would have 13 buses lined up in Moulsecoomb Way. Bring 'em all [the factory workers] here in the mornings and home again in the afternoons!' Mickey Webb thinks that the close proximity of factories was a major consideration in the location of the garage. Paul Williams agrees. 'In those days Southdown operated mainly the routes in that area of town, to such places as East Moulsecoomb, Coldean, Lower Bevendean, and so, from a mileage point of view, it was a good place to have a garage. It was easy to get to Coldean or those other areas for starting a journey first thing in the morning or to finish there late at night. So it actually

saved the mileage of having to take the bus back into the centre of Brighton.'

When Mickey first started at Moulsecoomb it was an all crewed garage: drivers and conductors. In a relatively short space of time that position had changed. 'In the years that followed I had a 'half-and-half' garage,' he remembered, 'part crewed and part one-man, which slightly cut down our original vehicle capacity.' He explained that before the advent of the one-man operator bus [driver/conductor or D/C as it became known in Southdown], Moulsecoomb had housed 30 vehicles.

'We had six-cylinder and five-cylinder Guys', he recalled, 'and the old PD2 Leylands. Quite a few of the original 'open-backers' were there, but a year after I took over they started bringing in those with the doors on the back.' Thinking back, he remembered two versions of those: 'We had the folding rear door and the sliding one. The PD3 chassis with what was known as the 'Queen Mary' body came next; these were getting on for nine-foot wide with the mirrors and they took up a lot of space.' The 30 buses at Moulsecoomb were reduced once the newer Driver/Conductor buses appeared. Mickey commented that, 'when they started bringing in things like Daimlers I ended up with 25 buses.'

'The main changes I saw,' said Webb, 'were the crew buses converting to the one-man type. Initially these were conversions of PD3s, but the purpose-built buses like the Atlanteans, the Bristol VRs and Nationals which were really built for the job, started to appear. Most of our Leyland Leopards also, were delivered with a one-man cab already in place. Of course the other big change was Southdown yo-yoing from a private to a nationalised company, and then back again.'

Mickey Webb joined Southdown after serving 12 years in the RAF, and as such wanted to foster a similar esprit de corps at the garage. He realised that as drivers were arriving from about 04.15 it might be an idea to organise a tea fund, and thus ensure a nice hot 'cuppa' for those cold dark mornings. He said, 'We bought a book and everyone paid a shilling [5p] a week.' The fund guaranteed a supply of tea, sugar, milk etc. Mick smiled: 'Well, we did this for a while and obviously we started to show a profit. So I had a word with the lads and said we've got this amount of money what shall we do with it?' The consensus was to buy some Premium Bonds.

'You would not believe it but on our first draw we won £50! I said the one thing we need is a fridge, so we went out and got one. Then we were able to keep things like eggs, bacon and loaves of bread. And that started the breakfasts rolling. Then, North Sea Gas conversion came along so we had a new cooker.'

Mickey Webb next went to the company and persuaded them to invest in a new gas boiler. The previous equipment was an old coke burner which was always out when Mickey arrived in the morning. And by the time it was roaring hot everyone had long gone! With the new boiler installed there was instant heat in the rest room and office; even first thing in the mornings. The 20th century had arrived.

'It helped everyone, particularly in winter months when it was cold. And having breakfast available for those that had come in early in the morning, I thought, was the right way to get people in the mood to go to work.

'Then I got on to top management and asked if they had any objections to me allowing staff on the early shift parking their cars inside the garage.' It was, of course, a move that ensured Mickey's staff would be there at work 'instead of tearing around Moulsecoomb looking for a place to park, because

require any anti-freeze.

'Well I fought against it and said that I thought this decision wrong because Moulsecoomb was one of the coldest places you could be in winter, and with no heating outside the offices and rest room, it was very, very cold.

'I was very proud that we rarely lost a service at MG, but on this particular day we lost dozens! There were buses frozen-up everywhere. Two had lost their engines up in Coldean. As soon as they had got up there and had warmed up they just burst; their cylinders split during the night because they had frozen solid. Anyway, I had a phone call from the general manager to say I had been proven right and anti-freeze would arrive the next morning.'

There were other degrees apart from the minus

Brighton council, in their wisdom, had stuck yellow lines the length of Moulsecoomb Way.'

With the on-site parking and early morning 'TLC' Mickey fostered a philosophy that worked: 'I issued everybody with a key and that also helped in the happy environment. I was pleased with the fact that I had a very happy garage.' In all those years Mickey Webb rarely lost a service. Except of course that winter.

A question of degrees.

Situated where it was, Moulsecoomb garage suffered from the cold during wintertime. This was not usually a problem for Southdown's well-maintained fleet. Not until a policy change. Mickey said, 'I don't want to criticise engineering management but some bright spark decided that as we had a turn around of less than six hours (between the last bus in at night and the first one out in the morning) we didn't

Approaching Brighton's Castle Square prior to commencing its north-bound trip to Lower Bevendean, Southdown Leyland National no.108 (AYJ 108T). It is probably a change-over just out of Edward Street garage, situated behind the white building on the left.

ones at Moulsecoomb Garage. The A27 that used to run alongside it also separates the campuses of the University of Brighton and the University of Sussex, and is known as the 'academic corridor'. Every June many graduates decide that the cosmopolitan lifestyle of Brighton is far too enthralling to leave behind, and feel compelled to stay. With the summer season just starting jobs were often to be found at Southdown and being near to their old campus ex-students would beat a path to the door at Moulsecoomb.

'One thing that was known throughout the

During 1978, weekend staff shortages at Conway Street led to some Moulsecoomb buses and drivers operating Conway Street duties. Here Moulsecoomb driver E R Shrubb waves to a colleague driving Bristol VRT no.571 (GNJ 571N) on a service 2 bus in Rottingdean's High Street.

Southdown company,' said Mickey, 'was that we had the largest number of people with degrees than any other depot. There wasn't top jobs for the graduates to go around, you see, so many of these educated people came and worked on the buses.'

This 'elitism' was further compounded by the fact that there was often a nine-month waiting-list for people choosing to transfer to Moulsecoomb garage. Drivers just wanted to work there, and the entire social spectrum was represented. Passing through those gates during my time for example was, an ex-dustman, an ex-teacher, a theology bachelor, a flying instructor, several cabbies, a guy who always wanted 'lates' because he was starting a building firm and numerous ex-servicemen including a RAF (retd) Flight Lieutenant. Mickey remembered him not least because they had held the same rank.

'Roger Hunt, I'll always remember him,' said Mickey laughing, 'One day he was doing a no.13 when I had a phone call from my manager wanting to know were this certain bus had got to. I told him that I hadn't had any reports or phone calls. He said: 'Well it has not turned up; it has gone missing between the Old Steine [Brighton's seafront terminus] and Coldean.' I found out later that because Roger was such an obliging chap and he had picked up an 'old dear' who lived up at Lower Bevendean who'd got on the wrong bus, that he'd

told her not to worry about it and ran her home! He went off route, dropped her off and had to go all around the estate's one-way loop and back again. By the time he reached Coldean he should have been back at the Old Steine for the next trip. Actually, he didn't last all that long because he wasn't cut out for the job; really nice bloke though.'

There were many characters, enough probably to fill a book. During my own time at the garage the one abiding memory I have is this feeling almost of belonging to a 'gentlemen's club'. In using that phrase I am not being overtly sexist because until my friend Lynda Hill joined the garage in 1980 it was still a male preserve. Having been an ex-serviceman, Mickey really did try to keep a sense of comradeship going. For example, if you were on an early 'turn', your duty was preceded by 20 minutes booking-on time. This was time to prepare your vehicle for use, screen up the correct destination blind, install the ticket machine, do a visual safety check and top up the radiator. A sort of 'gentlemen's agreement' evolved whereby the early 'spare' would 'top up' and visually check the vehicles, thus allowing a few extra minutes for the duty driver to have a cup of tea before going on the road. A good many of the drivers, however, would get in 20 minutes earlier in order to have breakfast as well. Such was the spirit of the place that it was almost pleasurable to be there – even at 05.30.

Whither Moulsecoomb?

When Southdown first operated its services from the garage, along with the town routes were several country services. Runs to East Grinstead, Chelwood Gate, Hawkhurst and Haywards Heath started from Moulsecoomb. Over time, and drops in passenger numbers, these routes disappeared or were taken over by the likes of London Country. And again when Southdown merged into NBC a number of other routes were lost. Worse was to come as the 1970s flipped into the 1980s and car ownership in Brighton reached new heights. Even the successful town routes started to suffer. As Mickey Webb lamented: 'The frequency of services dropped according to passenger numbers and obviously some routes didn't require quite so many buses. Where we were running a quarter-of-an-hour frequency it went to just half-an-hour – so you could afford to lose one or more buses per route. Well, you do that over the entire company and you're losing a lot of vehicles.' Following privatisation, an amalgamation of services with Conway Street began and vehicles started to park at the coach garage at Freshfield Road.

Southdown Queen Mary 834 (VUF 834) shares the road with a Brighton, Hove & District Bristol K5G and a Brighton Corporation AEC Regent/Weymann in 1958 – note the trolleybus wiring.
Michael Dryhurst

The end for Moulsecoomb, as Mickey reflected, was in sight. 'Steine Street – the coastal express station – was shut; Edward Street garage was closed down and the buses were moved out of Pool Valley. There just weren't the services. The Moulsecoomb buses started to be parked in Whitehawk and Conway Street. Conway had the capacity because of its two garages and could therefore, take the load.'

In the late 1984 Mickey Webb left Moulsecoomb garage to work from a garage inspectors' office in Conway Street. Within six months of that the Moulsecoomb site ceased to operate as a bus garage. So now the milk is stored there, but unlike the garage at Edward Street and the coach depot of Steine Street it does remain intact to illustrate its part in the history of passenger transport. The others are lost to us forever: Steine Street is a BT office block and Edward Street a developed but ever unused

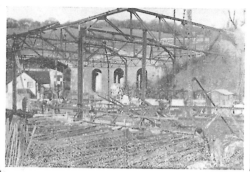 

Last news of Moulscombe garage, in November, was of the clearing of the site.   By now, as will be seen, progress has been made on the actual construction.

Above: *Two photos from The Southdown Chronicle, March 1957, show construction work under way at 'Moulscombe' garage.*

Below: *Also from The Southdown Chronicle, in this case the Summer 1969 issue, a one-person-operated Leyland Leopard PSU3/1R with Weymann bodywork bound for Angmering at Worthing seafront.*

"CONNECTIONS

WILL

BE

MADE

AT . . . ."

No. 7

WORTHING

There are very few advertised connections featured in Southdown's time... are centred in one of the ... the area, ...

... half-hourl... ...he 31 has be...

vacant office complex: quite ugly.

The story however, is not completely finished and a certain mystery remains. There appears to be a clash of views between Paul Williams and Mickey Webb as to who actually owns Moulsecoomb garage. Mickey Webb seemed to think that Brighton & Hove Buses still own it and that buses might move back there.

Paul Williams will not be drawn any further, except to say that he cannot foresee it ever being used again as a bus depot: 'Even if we were able to buy it back – which is not necessarily feasible because it's used as a dairy at the moment – I can't see that we'd ever use it again. To be honest it's fairly small for a town garage.' He added, 'Although we are full up at Conway Street and Whitehawk it's going to

a while before we exhaust capacity at Lewes Road.'

I will finish by saying that if you asked for a comment from any of its crews over the years, the response would mostly be the same: it was a good place to work. I will leave the question of ownership open to conjecture but would like to throw in this final conundrum: if the Go-Ahead Group now owns the nearby Metrobus – whose own success in route accumulation has made its small yard in Lewes groan under the strain of an increased vehicle allocation – might we yet see Metrobus and stablemates Brighton & Hove rethinking the Moulsecoomb equation? Whatever happens I would like to think that Moulsecoomb garage could yet have another 15 minutes of fame.   **CB**

DAY TRIP TC

In July 1963 C B GOLDING set off for Bradford with his camera

Above: *The Bradford Corporation trolleybus system was still sizeable in the summer of 1963; one route had been abandoned in 1962 and the withdrawal of the Crossflatts trolleybuses later in 1963 would rob the system of some of its vehicle variety. Withdrawn later in 1963 was Weymann-bodied no.810 (BDY 800), one of 12 1948 Sunbeam W bought from Hastings Tramways in 1959; this one has Park Royal 56-seat bodywork. It is seen outside Thornbury garage passing 1950 AEC Regent III/ Weymann motorbus no.26 (FKY 26).* All photos by C B Golding

Right: *Thornbury garage again, and no.750 (EKU 750), a 1949 BUT 9611T with 58-seat Roe body, new to Bradford.*

BRADFORD

Above: *In its final years the Bradford trolleybus fleet was augmented by secondhand examples from systems around the country – Ashton, Brighton, Darlington, Doncaster, Grimsby, Hastings, Llanelly, Mexborough & Swinton, Notts & Derby and St Helens. No.764 (NNU 228), a 1949 BUT 9611T/Weymann 58-seater, came from Notts & Derby in 1953.*

Right: *Bought from South Wales Transport this 1945 ex-Llanelly & District Karrier W, no.778 (CBX 601), was placed in service in Bradford in 1956 with this new 63-seat East Lancs body. It is seen leaving Thornbury garage.*

Above: *No.801 (BDJ 89) was one of eight 1951 BUT 9611T with East Lancs 63-seat bodies bought from St Helens Corporation and placed in service in Bradford in 1959.*

Below: *Leaving Thornbury garage is no.634 (BAK 934), a 1937 AEC 661T with 1956 East Lancs 63-seat body.*

Left: *Used latterly as a driver training bus, no.060 (KY 8200) was an AEC 661T new in 1934 and rebodied by Northern Coachbuilders after the war. It is shown approaching Thornbury garage.*

Below: *Newly rebodied by East Lancs in 1963 with this 66-seat forward entrance body, Sunbeam F4 no.844 (FWX 914) was new to Mexborough & Swinton in 1948 as a single-decker. These buses survived to the end of the Bradford trolleybus system – the last in the UK – in March 1972, and no.844 was the official last trolleybus to operate in Bradford and in the UK.*

No1: Glasgow Corporation's Daimlers

When? November 1937 to May 1975

How many? 436, of which all but 44 were double-deck and all but 30 (trolleybuses before you imagine otherwise) were diesels.

Why were they bought? After standardising on Leylands, AECs and some locally-made Albions, Glasgow turned to Daimler for 25 Weymann-bodied COG6s it needed to beef up its fleet to handle crowds expected to attend the 1938 Empire Exhibition in the city.

A momentous event? Yes, and it took another one to prompt the purchase of its next 69 Daimlers. Like World War 2. Glasgow's need for utilities was less in the earlier stages of the war than in other parts of the country. The exhibition had boosted and modernised its fleet and the west of Scotland was beyond practical range of the Luftwaffe for more than a handful of exceptional air raids. Nineteen Guys were followed from 1943 by 62 AEC 7.7-litre CWA6s, five Daimler CD6-engined CWD6s and just two more sluggish Gardner 5LW-powered CWG5s. Thirty CWA6s were rebodied by East Lancs in 1954 and gave another eight years' passenger service.

So Glasgow was hooked on Daimlers after the war? Not to the exclusion of everything else, but it liked them well enough to buy 341 between 1948 and 1959 – more than any other single make over that key period when it renewed its fleet and began replacing trams. Of these, 195 came with Gardner 6LWs, 113 had CD6s, three had CD650-family Daimler engines and 30 were six-wheel trolleybuses with Metro-Cammell bodies to London Transport's Q1 design. Or at least you might think the city bought more than of any other make.

Why do you backtrack so? Over the same period, it got

286 Leylands, 266 AECs, 124 Albions, plus 144 BUT and 20 Sunbeam trolleybuses. But if you class 123 of the BUTs as AECs and 21 as Leylands (the manufacturers that actually made them), then AEC out-built Daimler by a small margin – 389 to 341.

Did Weymann enjoy the same follow-through of body orders as Daimler did from the first COG6s? Not on Daimler chassis, of which it only bodied nine utilities and 49 CVG6s supplied in 1955. Five of the utilities were among the 30 rebodied by East Lancs. It did body lots of AEC Regents and a few Regals.

So who bodied the rest? Alexander supplied 214 between 1950 and 1963, Brush built 45 utilities, Glasgow Corporation itself assembled 43 dual-door single-deckers from Metal Sections kits between 1948 and 1952, while there were 20 Northern Coachbuilders-bodied CVD6s, nine Duple utilities, five Scottish Aviation CVD6s, three utilities each from Massey and Northern Counties and one CVD6 from Mann Egerton. Brush, incidentally, bodied all the CWD6s while Massey's trio included both CWG5s; 19 of the rebuilds originally had Brush bodies. Two of the Alexander bodies went on to second chassis.

Eh? In 1960, the solitary CD650 chassis was scrapped and its body replaced the solitary scrapped Mann Egerton body, both of which were 8ft wide. The following year saw a 7ft 6in Alexander body move from a scrapped chassis on to the chassis which previously sat beneath an NCB body.

Why solitary CD650 when you said something earlier about three? The others were a 1953 Freeline with horizontal D650H engine and a 1957 CVD650-30. There also were five 1959 double-deckers with late-model CD6s, semi-automatic gearboxes and Manchester-style fronts. And in case you wondered how we got to a total of 436, a solitary Fleetline was delivered in May 1963 for comparison with hundreds of Atlanteans. It was the only Daimler Glasgow bought after Jaguar acquired the company from BSA. A Glasgow-spec, Glasgow-liveried Fleetline appeared at the following November's Scottish Motor Show but became demonstrator 565 CRW, repainted red and white.

The strangest Glasgow Daimler fact? Perhaps that the highest-numbered of the 43 GCT-bodied single-deckers, DS43, was built nine months before any of the others, which started with DS1 and took over four years to reach DS42. DS43 also had by far the highest chassis number of the batch.

Alan Millar

D225 (SGD 208), one of 45 CVG6s with Alexander bodies, Manchester bonnets and semi-automatic gearboxes supplied in 1959 along with five similar CVD6s.
Alan Millar

THE KEYNOTE is *Elegance*

G E HAWKYARD recalls the Middlesex-based coachbuilder, Whitson

DESPITE a relatively brief existence of less than 20 years, the bodybuilding business of James Whitson & Company Limited succeeded in producing a wide range of coaches, buses and commercial vehicles which continue to arouse much interest amongst enthusiasts even some 50 years after production ceased.

I joined the company in September 1951 when the business had been going for some five years and was based at a factory adjacent to the junction of Sipson Lane and the Bath Road in West Middlesex directly opposite the original North Entrance to Heathrow Airport. This was then a collection of pre-fabricated sheds; the massive 'city' with which we are now familiar was still a planners dream.

The leading light behind James Whitson was Alfred Whittit, a

stocky, forthright northerner born and brought up in Hendon near Sunderland. Between the two World Wars, Alf and his brother Harry worked together at several coachbuilding companies including Strachans Successors at North Acton and Dennis Brothers in Guildford where Alf held a managerial position in the bodyshop at the outbreak of World War 2. He was astute enough to realise that hostilities would present an opportunity to strike out on his own and he set up H&S Engineering which undertook small light engineering and machining contracts for government departments. This business was housed in an old barn adjacent to Harlington Corner on the Bath Road and Alf Whittit was joined in this venture by his brother Harry. This company prospered and formed the foundation for the coachbuilding

A touch of the Duple A-type in this 1948 Whitson advert showing a coach body on Tilling-Stevens KM6A7 chassis.

HAVE YOUR **COACHWORK** BY

JAMES WHITSON & CO LTD

COACHBUILDERS AND ENGINEERS

Registered Offices and Works :
SIPSON ROAD, SIPSON, WEST DRAYTON, MIDDX.
Telephone : West Drayton 2863-2953

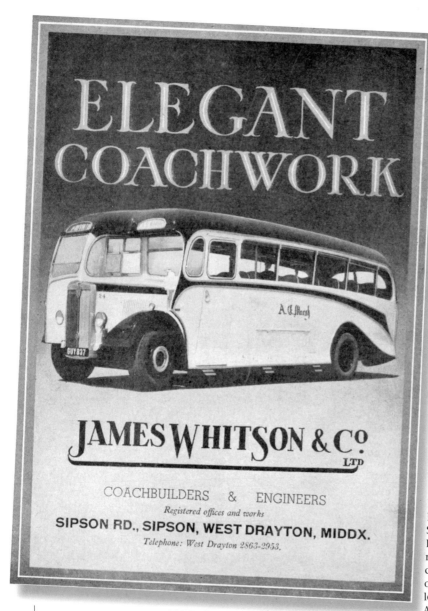

Similar coachwork fitted to a Maudslay Marathon in another 1948 advert.

of The Excelsior Hotel. The move into the new premises took place during 1952 and immediately enabled the company to undertake a greater volume of work.

Mundane

At the beginning, the coach designs from Whitson were mundane, to say the least, and coupled with the poor-quality timber which had had to be used, did little for its reputation. This was a time when operators were desperate to obtain any kind of vehicle to meet the postwar demand for leisure travel. There were many companies competing for custom and without reference to my records can recall such names as ACB, Metalcraft, Gurney Nutting, Pearsons of Liverpool, Portsmouth Aviation, Duple, Harrington, Santus, Dutfield, Burlingham, Thurgood, Strachans, Windover, Bellhouse Hartwell and many more, most of whom disappeared in the mid-1950s once the boom was over, now leaving only Plaxton and Alexander from those early days to fly the UK flag.

business immediately World War 2 was over. The H&S name survived into the Whitson era as the machine shop section of the main works.

Almost as soon as I joined the company, a compulsory purchase order had been issued to Mr Whittit on the grounds that the site was to form part of a planned extension to Heathrow. An inland lake for use by transatlantic flying boats was intended but the advent of larger land-based aircraft with stops in Iceland and Halifax Nova Scotia made travel to the USA easier and thus rendered this scheme redundant. However, on the strength of this order Whitson built a brand-new works at Yiewsley just north of West Drayton, Middlesex, on the main road to Uxbridge. The old Sipson Works was taken over by Hales Bread and eventually became the site

Construction of luxury coaches at that time was principally from timber with ash being used for the main framing and oak for the underframe, all reinforced with steel. All-metal coaches were still a little way off although for buses used on stage carriage work it was a different story as we shall see later. Most of the manufacturing was done 'in house' with the exception of windows, windscreens, louvres etc and signwriting. There was an extensive trimming department and an excellent paintshop which non-authorised staff entered on pain of death!

Whilst Alf Whittit was the leading light at Whitson, his brother Harry was the works manager. Many old colleagues from Strachans and Dennis joined the brothers and amongst them was one Charles Pilbin who was in charge of estimating and design in the early days. As I said earlier Whitson coach designs were not particularly stylish but all that changed when Alf took on Cyril Austin from Duple. He brought with him a wealth of experience and a flair for innovation which with Alf Whittit's sales ability really put Whitson on the map. Whitson design and quality immediately benefited from Cyril becoming chief draughtsman and the similarity between the Whitson halfcab 'FS 112' model and the then current Duple A-series was no accident. The one feature which made Whitson bodies stand out was the patented flush sliding door. This not only did away with the ugly recess necessitated by inside or outside sliding doors but also gave an attractive smooth flowing line to the nearside of the body. When front-engined chassis were the order of the day Whitson built on most available models but for some reason Crossley, Maudslay, Foden and Dennis seemed to predominate. Many of the smaller chassis were also bodied and these were often Austins and Commers since Duple appeared to have first call on the popular Bedford OB.

Innovative

Whitson was nothing if not innovative, and was always looking for new markets. Using the experience gained by the Whittit brothers at Dennis, several fire appliance contracts were dealt with including one of 77 units on Commer chassis for the Warwickshire Brigade. Many bodies were built under sub-contract for Sun Engineering on the Thornycroft Nubian chassis for Air Force and airport use as well as smaller Ford-based examples for the Fire Armour company. When I came to Whitson, they had one of their senior draughtsmen seconded to the Home Office with representatives of Windover and Willowbrook to prepare the drawings for the now-famous 'Green Goddess' fire appliance. These three built prototypes and Whitson was then involved in building a large number of the production models on both Bedford 4x2 and 4x4 chassis. The new factory

STARS OF THE SHOWS
NICE • NEW YORK • PARIS

A bright and particular star at Nice last year was this Whitson-Foden 30 ft. Luxury Touring Coach. Seating 37 passengers in air conditioned comfort, this coach was awarded L'Etoile d'Azur du Sydicat d'Initiatives

Skilfully built with prize winning grace, the Whitson Full Luxury Observation Coach has contributed magnificently to this story of success after success in the International field. Mounted on a Foden 2-stroke oil-engine chassis, and seating 35 passengers, this coach is the Grand Prix model so triumphantly shown at Nice and New York

Judged the most 'elegant coach of the 1950 Paris Motor Show, the Whitson 39-seater Luxury Coach, mounted on a Foden 2-stroke rear engined chassis, was awarded the First Prize and Diploma in its own class—a fitting reward for British supremity in design and craftsmanship

The Patented FLUSH-FITTING DOOR is an exclusive WHITSON Feature...

James WHITSON & Co. Ltd

SIPSON • WEST DRAYTON

Telephone: West Drayton 2863-2953

A confident Whitson advert from 1951 showing a Foden 37-seat coach, a 35-seat Foden Observation Coach for Salopia and a 39-seat rear-engined Foden, again for Salopia.

was well laid out and lent itself very well to flowline production of this sort. I confess that at the time I was involved with producing some of the works drawings for these vehicles I did not think that they would still be around 50 years later! In fact almost 1,000 are in store only a few miles from where I live.

Pride of place in the product line up was the famous 'Observation Coach' which was a one-and-a-half deck design giving much appreciated additional luggage space beneath the raised rear floor. Similar bodies had been produced by Duple and others

but these were the first stylish examples of a design forever immortalised by the Dinky Toy Maudslay. Alf Whittit took one of these, based on a full-fronted front-engined Foden chassis, to the 1950 New York Motor Show and received several awards and much

This 1952 advert shows a 39-seat rear-engined Foden Observation coach, Salopia again, and an AEC Regal IV 41-seater.

publicity. More important the company got an order from the United States Air Force for 12 similar units based on Crossley SD42 chassis and did other work for the USAF including some Austin-based service buses which could be easily converted into ambulances.

My arrival at Whitson coincided with the introduction of the underfloor-engined chassis in the form of the AEC Regal IV and the Leyland Royal

More unusual fare features in this 1953 Whitson advert – a rebodied AEC Regal 35-seater and a 25-seat normal control Commer for export to Cyprus.

Tiger. Foden offered the rear-engined format as its contribution to this change in chassis layout but the transverse engine layout did not find favour and was

The prototype Rutland Clipper rear-engined coach with Whitson bodywork.

ahead of its time for the conservative UK operator.

Amongst Cyril Austin's innovations was the early introduction of 'whale mouth' wrap-around windscreens and the dropping down of the screen waistrail in relation to the main bodyside waist. Early coach bodywork for underfloor-engined chassis tended to be an adaptation of existing front-engined designs and in fact this new Whitson styling originated with a design produced by Cyril Austin for his friend and neighbour Don Try of Windsorian Coaches who were based in Windsor, close to Cyril's home. This vehicle was built by Windsorian with help from Cyril and based on an early Dennis Lancet chassis, The vehicle, built in 1949 or 1950, was used in advertisements for Spandit windscreens and rubber glazing by The Empire Rubber Co for several years being quite an eye-catcher at that time. At that time the Construction and Use regulations stipulated that the driver of a public service vehicle should be able to see the road 70ft ahead without looking through glass. Thus all windscreens had to have an opening section which tended to stifle design somewhat. Another feature promoted by Whitson was the removal of the side 'flash' moulding which it replaced with five rows of polished aluminium, this well before the famous 'Happich' range of decorations became popular.

All-metal

Cyril left Whitson for 12 months in 1951 and spent that time with Brush Coachworks at Loughborough learning much about all-metal construction. He returned in 1952 to the new works and was my boss for some while. Whilst being a very strict disciplinarian, he was a good teacher and we

remained friends after I left right up until his early death from cancer at the age of 44.

Although much of the production capacity at the Yiewsley Works was taken up with building the Green Goddesses, there was still time for the regular customers. These included Salopia Saloon Coaches of Whitchurch which usually had one or two vehicles annually and frequently provided a display exhibit for the Whitson stand at the SMMT Commercial Motor Show at Earls Court on alternate years. In 1953, Maurice Rowe of M. G. Rowe Garages, Dobwalls, Cornwall, drove into the yard with what turned out to be the prototype Rowe Hillmaster. This centre-engine chassis had been built by Rowe, and Whitson put a neat coach body on to it. Rowe exhibited the completed vehicle in the car park at the 1954 Commercial Show and I believe that this was the only Rowe chassis fitted with a coach body. In 1954 another prototype to come to Whitson was the Rutland Clipper, a rear-engine chassis produced by Motor Traction Ltd (MTN) of Addington. This had a Perkins P6 engine positioned longitudinally and a second chassis had the later R6 engine. It was not a great success and had a tendency to come to the boil! The first vehicle was too heavy and the second body had several changes to improve the situation including an air duct down the rear. The first example went into service with H. W. Crouch's West Kent Coachways and the second went to Acorn Motors.

One of the most unusual vehicles produced during my time was a 12-seat minibus which was chassisless

Two Noteworthy Whitson Models!

The refinements which Whitson customers have come to expect from them are present in full complement in this latest 41-seater Luxury Coach, supplied to Messrs. G. R. & F. Longstaff, of North Broomhill, Morpeth. Mounted on a Sentinel chassis, the coach is fitted with heater, radio, de-misters and air ventilation, and is an outstanding example of elegance combined with economy.

The Model illustrated alongside is yet another example of superb design by Whitsons, combining streamlined beauty with essential practicality. It is a 44-seater service bus on a Sentinel underfloor engine chassis.

James WHITSON & Co., Ltd.

YIEWSLEY · WEST DRAYTON · MIDDLX.

Telephones : West Drayton 2863 & 2953

Whitson built on Sentinel chassis – this 1955 advert features a 41-seat SLC6 coach for Longstaffs of Morpeth and a 44-seat bus to Beadle design for Reliance, Great Gonersby.

the standard 44-seat bus body, although this was a Beadle look-alike, no drawings or other information was provided by Sentinel and the finished product was almost impossible to distinguish from the original. Reliance of Great Gonerby had one of these There was much work at that time 'modernising' older halfcab coaches by incorporating a full front with wrap-around screens. There was also a regular order from Solomonides in Cyprus who ordered service bus bodywork on Commer Superpoise chassis to a 1930s design!

The last SMMT show at which I did stand duty for Whitson included a Sentinel coach for H. Best and Son, which had the last three rows of seats facing the rear with a large panoramic window. The idea did not catch on however and probably caused travel sickness amongst the rear-facing passengers. At the 1952 show was the last of the famous Observation Coaches. This was another Foden for Salopia but this body was unique in having a clerestory roof profile which was I believe an attempt to reduce the height if only in appearance!

By the time I left and went to Spurlings at Hendon in the mid-1950s, the luxury coachbuilding business was already in decline with Duple, Plaxton, Burlingham and Harrington dominating the industry.

In just a few short years, Whitson achieved a great deal and enjoyed a well-deserved reputation for quality and design. In those days individual operators' tastes could still be catered for without the cost being prohibitive.

and utilised a self-contained front-wheel drive diesel engine unit from Turner Manufacturing in Wolverhampton. This was intended to compete with the ubiquitous VW which at that time was still not universally admired here. Involvement with the government over the Green Goddess programme probably led to an order being obtained for 100 steel-framed buses on Bedford SB chassis. These were for use by the RAF and were readily convertible to stretcher carriers, this being the period when the Cold War was at its height.

Weight-conscious

Towards the end of my stay at Whitson most of the bodywork was on Foden or Sentinel chassis although both of these makes suffered from being too heavy at a time when operators were very weight-conscious. Several of the Sentinel STC6 chassis were bodied with

As a final chapter to this brief history, Mr D A T Grimmet, who joined Whitson after war service with the Royal Engineers, has kindly provided some information on the company's activities after I left.

Mr Grimmett was the buyer at Whitson whilst I was there and was involved until trading finally ceased in 1975. As the demand for buses and coaches declined, Whitson became more and more involved with glassfibre reinforced plastic mouldings both for its own use and for sale to other coachbuilders. Parts were produced for the Citroen Bijou (a UK stopgap for the 2CV), Coronet three-wheeled cars, Winchester London taxicabs, the prototype saloon car version of the Daimler Dart (which did not go into production), Peerless and Warwick cars which participated in the Monte Carlo Rally, Scammell Scarabs and other local delivery vans for British Railways. GRP cabs were also produced for Dennis

vehicles, (an instance of the wheel turning full circle for the Whittit family) and for AEC as well as domes etc for Park Royal Vehicles and C. H. Roe

Finally 27ft and 33ft cruiser hulls were manufactured for Progress River Cruisers and so even until the end Whitson was still involved in passenger carrying products.

Whilst not being a full history, I hope that this article has thrown some new light on one of the more successful postwar smaller coachbuilders whose products continue to interest the enthusiast. **CB**

At Brighton taking part in a British Coach Rally in the 1950s, what is thought to be the second Rutland Clipper with Whitson body – and although the position of the front axle and the 'R' logo have echoes of the Rowe Hillmaster, the lack of a front grille could support the Rutland theory. It is Acorn Motors 776 LMU.
Michael Dryhurst

CLASSIC WONDERBUS

THOSE OF YOU who already know the editor's own preferences might think this article is a blatant act of toadying, an endorsement of his belief that no bus can possibly be wonderful if it hasn't been built by Leyland. And that no Leyland is more wonderful than the Titan PD2.

Let me plead my case for objectivity. Regular readers of *Classic Bus* magazine will know, surely, that more than the occasional Leyland has warranted inclusion in the Classic Blunderbus series run in every issue since no.1 and I would also draw your attention to the makers of the Wonderbuses profiled since Yearbook 2 – Bristol, Leyland, Daimler, Guy and AEC. No huge bias in favour of Lancashire's biggest chassis builder. I have no hesitation in turning this year to the PD2, of which over 6,000 were built between 1947 and 1969. This was one of the true greats of British bus building, a volume-produced, honest, reliable classic bus operated by every class of operator at all ends of the country and overseas, too.

And don't just take my word for it. Geoffrey Hilditch, revered and now retired general manager and engineer in various municipal fleets, wrote in his *A Further Look at Buses* book of his first encounter with an early PD2 somewhere near Todmorden. He had already discovered the limitations of the stop-gap PD1 design and admits that while waiting his turn in a very long queue at a Pennine bus stop one Sunday afternoon, he was disheartened when he thought he was about to be ushered on to a PD1. 'There was, though, a slightly different engine note apparent as we took our places on the front nearside lower saloon seat, but then when we had about 20 standing we received the starting signal and a revelation.

'That bus, which was complete with a Leyland body, positively swept up the quite substantial gradients which lay between the town and our destination and I began to realise that this was one of the new O.600-engined buses that my chief had mentioned some time earlier in something that

A sight and sound for a desert island? South Notts no.48 (MRR 338), a lowbridge version of the final style of Leyland-bodied PD2, in Nottingham in 1973. Behind is one of the operator's Northern Counties-bodied Leyland Lowlanders.
Alan Millar

approached awed tones, and I by the end of the ride had come to the distinct conclusion that here was a machine that could outpace a Regent MkIII which was then rather dear to our hearts.'

The O.600 lay at the heart of the PD2's success. Developing 9.8 litres rather than the 7.4 litres of the E181 in the previous year's PD1, this new engine benefited from Leyland's wartime military experience and had been installed in truck chassis from 1946. Although seen as a long-term successor to the PD1, the new model was offered in parallel with it and it wasn't until 1952 that the last PD1s were supplied and there was even a one-off experimental PD2 with an E181 engine a few years later.

The PD2 hit the market just as fleets were being renewed after the lean years of World War 2, but its attractive specification made it a product of choice, rather than one of last or even second or third resort.

Right: What became the Midland Red front on the PD2 was first seen on the 100 Leyland-bodied 56-seat PD2s for Midland Red in 1952/3. Seen en route for Earls Court for the 1952 Commercial Motor Show is no.3978 (SHA 378).

Below: The Midland Red-style front on a PD2/20 married to a Willowbrook 63-seat body for The Delaine of Bourne, in that company's distinctive blue livery. This bus, KTL 780, is now preserved.

PD2s went into BET, SMT and municipal fleets. Only the odd one got into the Tilling fleets, most of which were directed to buy Bristols and were more likely to be told to wait for Bristols even if their immediate delivery requirements couldn't be met. Peculiarities in the ownership of Cumberland Motor Services meant it took Leylands into the state-owned era, including 52 PD2s bought between 1949 and 1952. And the ultimate achievement was for London Transport to buy 2,131 heavily modified PD2s between 1948 and 1954 – the RTL and RTW classes which married the standard Leyland chassis with the body, transmission, low bonnet line and outline requirements of the standard RT built around AEC's Regent MkIII.

If the RTL and RTW were the highest profile and least obviously Leyland of all PD2s – and remember that they accounted for a highly significant proportion of all sales of the family – the most typical model was the Leyland-bodied provincial version built until bus body production at Leyland came to an abrupt halt in 1954. Their handsomely proportioned bodies were evolved from prewar designs and, indeed, kept on evolving right up to the introduction of the final version in 1950 with rubber glazing and radiused window corners. To be unashamedly subjective, the combination of one of those final generation Leyland bodies – the design we mistakenly believed for decades was called the Farington when that was something else – and the hissing sound of its engine ticking over on idle encapsulates all that was best for me of early postwar buses. It's a memory I'd take happily to my desert island.

That alone should be sufficient to make it a Wonderbus, but it earns the accolade with knobs on for its chameleon-like adaptability to the changing world in which it operated. A 1952 order for 100 from Midland Red – its LD8 class – took it into the age of the concealed radiator, with a full-width bonnet and tin front modelled closely on that already developed for the operator's own BMMO D7 double-decker launched the following year. When Leyland started offering this bonnet assembly option to other customers from 1954, it even left space on all of them for the BMMO badge and didn't change the arrangement until the glassfibre St Helens-specification bonnet (with improved nearside kerb visibility) replaced it from 1960.

There were similar changes as permitted dimensions and transmission and braking requirements prompted additional models. Originally available as a 26ft long chassis in either 7ft 6in or 8ft widths, it grew to 27ft with the new length limit introduced in 1950 and was joined by the 30ft PD3 from 1956. The 7ft 6in versions were deleted from the manufacturer's catalogue from 1962, but were built to special order for a while longer, with Colchester buying them until 1964 and Warrington taking 12 28ft 5in by 7ft 6in models as late as 1965.

The PD2 family was exported as well. These are part of a 1957 batch of 50 OPD2/6 with 63-seat MCW Orion bodies supplied to Madrid. Note the right-hand driving position and platform.

Air brakes were available to special order from 1948, with 115 PD2/4 models going to Bolton and Bury and 100 centre-entrance PD2/5s for Blackpool before they became a standard option to vacuum brakes from 1950.

Although prewar Titans had been available with the option of Leyland's Gearless torque converter automatic transmission, the standard PD2 specification was a manual gearbox with synchromesh on all but first gear. Geoffrey Hilditch's praise for that Todmorden bus was leavened by subsequent experience of trying to locate first gear in a hurry, but most operators were prepared to live with it. London Transport's RTLs and RTWs all came with Wilson preselective gearboxes, as did 11 specially-built PD2/14s built for Leeds and Walsall in 1953/54.

By then, Leyland had developed its own Pneumo-Cyclic semi-automatic gearbox that became available as an option on all air-braked PD2s from 1954. While manual gearbox PD2s helped Leyland regain a strong foothold in the important Scottish municipal market by persuading Edinburgh to buy 371 vacuum-braked models between 1952 and 1962, it took the air brake/Pneumo-Cyclic combination to take the effect towards the west coast where Glasgow followed a 1955 batch of 25 7ft 6in-wide PD2/25s with 300 8ft-wide PD2/24s. Where other people's PD2s hissed and ground their way through the gears in classic fashion, these buses whined in the musical fashion of contemporary diesel multiple unit trains. Much smaller batches of similar buses went to Manchester and Swindon.

The PD2's final glory was to live long enough, despite the counter-attractions of both the bigger PD3 and the rear-engined Atlantean, to be bought into the earliest days of one-man operation of double-deckers. Indeed, the very last – a trio of F-suffixed, manual gearbox, forward-entrance East Lancs-bodied PD2/47s – went to Darwen Corporation, an operator which had followed Brighton's lead in 1966 when the south coast municipality had converted some half-cab PD2s for driver-only fare collection. One-man half-cabs may not have been an ideal solution, but they showed just how adaptable and potentially long lasting the PD2 could be. Why it deserves to be classed as one of the Wonderbuses. **CB**

Alan Millar

The St Helens front changed the appearance of the PD2. This PD2A/30 with 57-seat Massey body, no.80 (480 EFJ), was delivered to Exeter Corporation in 1962.
Gavin Booth

THE QUEST FOR ALUGUER

The famed Lost City? Well, no. The legendary Portuguese coachbuilder? Er, no. As GAVIN BOOTH discovered to his dismay, Aluguer is rather more prosaic

Climbing out of Lisbon's historic Alfama district in July 1987, two of RN's once-large AEC fleet, apparently bound for Aluguer. They are on private hire work – there's a clue here – and no.0154 (EN-28-27) is a 1976 UTIC-AEC U2075 with 73-seat(!) bodywork. All photos by Gavin Booth

I T WAS the destination on all of the most interesting coaches, and on my first visit to Portugal in 1985 I vowed that I would get myself there. They said they were going to ALUGUER, but then to confuse me they seemed to head off in every direction. I had sussed the Lisbon city services; it didn't seem to be a city terminus. I had inspected maps of the local rail system, but no luck there. I'd pored over guidebooks; no mention.

At least I didn't ask anyone in my faltering Portuguese where Aluguer was. It slowly dawned that this 'place', destination for all the most interesting coaches and therefore potentially worth a visit, was the Portuguese for 'On Hire' and these were just private hire coaches. Ah well. Fortunately Lisbon is ringed with real places offering as much vehicle variety as I had hoped to find at Aluguer, so all was not lost.

In 1985 Portugal was hardly uncharted territory for transport enthusiasts, but I got there in time to sample some of the delights that would quickly disappear. I must confess that I knew little about what to expect there. My parents had already enjoyed a holiday on the Estoril Coast, just outside Lisbon, and had persuaded us to join them there. We

Once out of the centre of Lisbon, the Carris AEC
Regent Vs found them in some difficult terrain. In this
1987 view, a 1960s Regent climbs towards the
terminus at Marvila on the 39 route, the last
stronghold of the type.

British roots

Carris, the Lisbon municipal operator, had
British roots and when it bought its first
serious motorbuses these were AEC
Regents that entered service after World
War 2. The AEC connection continued
into the 1960s, with Regals, Regents and
Reliances, but from the 1970s Volvo, Iveco
and MAN chassis were favoured, with
Mercedes-Benz the current favourite. The
Carris Regals soldiered on for a few more
years on services where full-size single-
deckers couldn't be used; they were first
replaced by the Daimler CVUs, but these
in turn gave way to midi-size MANs in the
1990s.

The remaining Regent Vs survived into
the 1990s, looking decidedly battle-worn,
and they were replaced by Fleetlines and
then by midi-size single-deckers. Some
Fleetlines survive as open-toppers for city
sightseeing, but their days must be
numbered as Carris is rebodying Volvo
B59s with new Camo open-top double-
deck bodies.

were staying in the delightful seaside town of
Cascais, terminus of the electric railway to Lisbon,
and while Cascais offered AECs and Volvos from the
nationalised Rodoviária Nacional (RN) fleet our first
trip into Lisbon was an eye-opener. I can still
remember stepping out into the 85deg sun at Cais do
Sodré station and marvelling at the sight that met
me. Trams of all shapes and sizes, some clearly very
old, and – wasn't that a halfcab mirror-image AEC
Regal over there? It was, and there was more to
come. A walk along the banks of the Tagus led to
Praça Comércio, where there were more Regals, a
British-sounding single-decker that turned out to be
a Daimler CVU (well, actually a Guy Victory in
disguise), and, yes, double-deckers.

The first I saw was a Daimler Fleetline with a
Weymann-esque body, and just as I was taking this
in, a well-laden AEC Regent V with similar bodywork
lurched into view. I was going to like this place!

Not only that but the local toyshops sold Metosul
Leyland Atlanteans, a slightly crude left-hand drive
adaptation of the earliest Dinky Toys model, and
available in a range of current and older liveries.
Needless to say, I bought as many of these as I could
– but wish I'd bought more, because on subsequent
trips Metosul products had disappeared.

AEC's man in Portugal must have been
working very hard in the postwar years. Not only did
he sell double-deckers into the Lisbon municipal
fleet, he convinced Coimbra and Porto that they
needed some as well. And in between times he seems
to have sewn up RN's bulk orders and impressed
many of the remaining independents. So much so
that there are still hundreds of AECs to be found
throughout Portugal. OK, a decade ago there were
thousands of them, but as the newest ones are at
least 20 years old, it's hardly surprising. Not that the
age of a bus is any guide, for many Portuguese AECs
have been rebuilt, often with Volvo engines, and
rebodied.

AEC had set up a local assembly plant in Vila Nova
de Gaia with the operators' co-operative, UTIC, and
from Monocoaches and Reliances right through to
sets of Swift 760 units that were incorporated into
integral rear-engined coaches, often with
synchromesh gearboxes.

Other British manufacturers got a bit of a look in –
notably Bedford, Daimler and Guy – and some of
their exports could still be seen in the 1980s. Leyland
had supplied Worldmasters and Atlanteans to Porto,
and independents had bought Atlanteans for services
across the newly opened Ponte 25 de Abril
suspension bridge. BUT, the joint AEC/Leyland

venture, had supplied trolleybuses to Coimbra and Porto. Leyland continued to co-operate with UTIC after the closure of AEC, but the Portuguese market today is dominated by the big European players.

Sacrilege

The modern-day scene in Portugal is still fascinating – but it may be sacrilege to admit that in a book about classic buses, so I'll try to concentrate on what CB readers still beat a path to Portugal to see – the older British-made buses.

Where once you fell over AECs at every turn, today you have to go out and look for them. But there are still concentrations of – I was going to say Southall products, but they're more likely to be Vila Nova de Gaia products built around a Southall heart (maybe with a little input from Gothenburg).

And what about the bodywork on these AECs? In recent years Portuguese bodywork has gone, well, European – on one hand slightly bland, on the other perfectly acceptable to operators beyond Portugal. Look at Salvador Caetano, for instance, the best-known Portuguese coachbuilders in the UK. When the first Caetano bodies came to the UK in the late 1960s they were – how to put this delicately? – fairly garish. For readers with longer memories, they carried on the tradition of Yeates bodies of the 1950s, and were heavy on the chrome and sparing on the styling. The quality of Caetano bodies was never in question, but the Portuguese, like their Spanish neighbours, liked flashy coach bodies. Today, Caetano's Enigma range is

as restrained and stylish as anything else on the market – perhaps (whisper it) more restrained and stylish than some of the market leaders.

Salvador Caetano – not to be confused with Alfredo Caetano – is well represented in its home market, but the bodybuilders' badges on coaches reveal that there are or were a lot of smaller cottage industry-type coachbuilders, as well as names that appear more regularly, like the aforementioned Alfredo C, and builders who had the capacity to supply the service bus market as well as dabbling – with varying degrees of success – in the coach market, like UTIC and Camo.

Exotic coaches

The place to see exotic coaches used to be Porto. Like so many other second cities Porto is a fine, hard-working, confident place, and the tentacles of the former RN national bus company never quite reached this far north. RN was set up after the 1974 bloodless revolution that restored democracy to Portugal, but only involved compulsory purchase of bus operators with 60 or more vehicles. While some independents around Lisbon managed to survive, most of the Porto area operators must have kept

their fleet size below 59, for one of the great bus sights was (and still is) the exodus of buses and coaches early every evening from the bus station and from a multitude of on-street termini. These buses – as mixed a bunch as you could hope for – mostly headed south out of the city across the imposing Dom Luis bridge across the Douro into the neighbouring town of Vila Nova de Gaia. The last time I was there, in 1998, I stayed in a hotel in Vila Nova de Gaia on the long Avenida da República sweeping down to the bridge and Porto. The centre of the road is a busway with bus stops at junctions; in other countries this would be a tramway, but it is fascinating to watch the sheer volume of passengers that can be moved by bus. Once upon a time, of course, it was a tramway, and on my first visits to the area it was served by Porto trolleybuses.

The independents still offer an amazing variety of buses. Elderly AECs and Volvos vie with newer types. For a time after the supply of AECs dried up, Portuguese operators turned to their wealthier European partners and eagerly snapped up buses that had been prematurely replaced. So you found Dutch standard DAF MB200s, for instance, or MANs and Mercs from German municipalities.

Exciting

On my early visits to Portugal, the Porto municipal fleet, STCP, was every bit as exciting as the Carris fleet in Lisbon. It offered motorbuses, trams and trolleybuses, and if that were not enough excitement, some of the motorbuses were Leylands (gasp!), and some of the trolleybuses were double-deckers.

There were Worldmasters, disguised beneath Portuguese bodies, and identified only by the badging or by the O.680 engine sound. The Atlanteans were less of a problem. There were older ones with Dalfa bodies, very British looking, or magnificent newer examples with stunning Caetano bodies which ran on long routes around the city.

The trolleybuses were something else – a mix of BUT single-deckers with Park Royal-styled UTIC bodies dating from the start of the trolleybus system in 1959/60, and 75 Lancias bought in 1967/8. Fifty of the Lancias were double-deckers with Dalfa bodies, and were used on two amazing, almost interurban, routes that went way out of the city, route 12 to the town of Gondomar and route 11 to the coal-mining area of S Pedro da Cova. STCP bought more new trolleybuses in 1986, but the system was quietly abandoned although the newest buses still apparently survive, and may possibly restart some day. This is a very Portuguese way of doing things, and the Porto tramway has been reduced to just one route which runs away from the city centre and

Above: *Vintage delights in Lisbon in July 1985. Carris 1948 AEC Regal III/ Weymann no.117 (FF-14-34) at Alfândega alongside Brill-built bogie car no.342, new in 1906.*

Left: *Carris AEC Regent V no.669 (CB-77-80) of 1965 sweeps down Lisbon's Avenida da Liberdade in July 1985. Note the Weymann-style UTIC forward entrance body, complete with outswept skirt.*

which casual visitors might have difficulty finding. It terminates at the fine Porto tramway museum – or rather, it did last time I was there. It could all have changed even if I had been there last week. The Museu do Carro Eléctrico is at Alameda Basilio Teles 51, on the banks of the Douro. STCP has a fine collection of older motorbuses and trolleybuses, but sadly these are not presently on public display.

North of Porto, by bus or narrow-gauge train, are towns which are served by an amazing selection of operators. Braga is a fine city with its own municipal buses and a busy bus station. Guimaraes has gained an undercover bus station. Famalicão has a vast open bus station, which, even on the hottest day of our 1998 trip, was still a place of pilgrimage for AEC fans. Barcelos is another busy place, particularly on market day, when locals pour in from the surrounding villages. But hurry if you want AECs. Arriva has arrived in Northen Portugal, so fleet replacement may be on the cards.

Coimbra

I only know the area between Porto and Lisbon from the comfort of a broad-gauge train – other than the university city of Coimbra. Roughly halfway between the main cities, this is a civilised place that at the time of my 1991 visit boasted both motorbuses and trolleybuses, though the trolleybuses have since gone. It also has a small tramway museum, a well-kept secret unless you know where to look and where to ask.

Most British holidaymakers head to the southern shores of the Algarve, and our one holiday there,

Left: *After squeezing its way down from Castelo de S Jorge in September 1988, Carris Daimler CVU no.76 joins the legendary 28 tram route for its descent into the centre of Lisbon and meets four-wheel tram no.745.*

Below: *Although most Carris Daimler Fleetlines ran in the standard orange/white livery, some for the airport service carried this Linha Verde (green line) scheme. No.822 (HL-45-14) of 1967, with Weymann-style Carris body, at Praça Comércio in November 1990.*

Above: *Portugal's first trolleybus route opened in Coimbra in 1947. This 1965 Sunbeam MF2B with UTIC bodywork was one of the last Sunbeams built for any customer. It is seen in September 1991.*

Below: *Porto started running trolleybuses in 1959 using 20 BUT LETB1 with UTIC bodies built under Park Royal licence. Thirty-one year old STCP no.17 is seen in May 1990.*

based at Lagos, revealed that there was still vehicle variety and, yes, there were still AECs to be found.

But the Lisbon area still has the edge – if only for the trams. If the Carris bus scene is missing the AECs and Daimlers, the trams more than make up for this. A once-comprehensive tramway system has been reduced to a mere handful of routes, served by two basic type of tram. The long coastal route, the 15, once the domain of splendid 90-year old bogie cars, is now dominated by ten new 24m long lowfloor articulated cars, the *Articulados*, bought in 1995. It's a wonderful route and passes the main STCP tram

Above: *In 1967/8 STCP (Porto) bought 75 Dalfa-bodied Lancia trolleybuses, including 50 two-door/two-staircase double-deckers. No.138, reaching the centre of Porto in May 1990 after its interurban trip from Gondomar, seems well-laden downstairs but the upper deck is strangely empty.*

Left: *Still running in the turquoise/cream livery in July 1985, STCP no.233, a Leyland Atlantean LPDR1/1 with Dalfa body, one of 30 bought in 1963/4.*

Left: *STCP bought a further 90 Atlanteans in 1966. These had O.680 engines and front-mounted radiators, and the stylish 32ft 7in long bodies were by built by Salvador Caetano in nearby Vila Nova de Gaia. No.268 (MO-72-44) is seen at Castelo do Queijo in May 1990 alongside a 1930-built 'Bogie Fumista' tram.*

Below: *A sawn-off reconstructed 1957 AEC Monocoach 2MC3LA with UTIC body in the fleet of Sequeira Lucas e Ventura, no.12 (BD-96-89) sits in Porto in May 1990 ready for the evening rush.*

depot at Santo Amaro, home of the Museu da Carris museum, which displays buses and trams from the city fleet.

The other trams are little four-wheel cars, the *Remodelados*. These ostensibly date from the 1930s but in the 1990s were extensively rebuilt to be thoroughly modern mechanically while still looking like a Lisbon tram should. Although there are heritage tram tours in slightly over-decorated preserved cars, forget them and buy a day ticket which gives you the buses and trams, and take an end-to-end trip on the legendary 28 route. This has some breathtaking switchback sections, and passes through streets so narrow that you can stretch out and touch the walls of the houses. I know this is a bus book, but surely even the most avid busfan would admit that Lisbon's trams are among the great transport experiences the world has to offer.

Still variety

If Lisbon's buses are not as varied as they were a decade ago, there is still variety to be found at the

bus stations that ring the city, pushed further out by the expanding Lisbon Metro. Worth visiting are Campo Grande and Praça de Espanha, the latter for buses heading across the impressive Ponte 25 de Abril bridge to the towns south of the Tagus. A railway has now opened using the lower deck of the 25 Abril bridge, but the regular ferries are worth a trip to see the variety offered in places like Cacilhas, and to admire the Lisbon skyline as you return.

West of Lisbon the regular electric trains take you to Estoril and Cascais, attractive holiday resorts with the added attraction for UK visitors of Stagecoach buses. Stagecoach Portugal was set up in 1996 when

Top: Northern Portuguese exotica – a 1955 AEC-engined Fiat with 1970 UTIC body, no.29 (RN-14-48) in the brightly-liveried fleet – complete with whitewall tyres – of João Carlos Soares e Filhos, seen at Guimaraes in May 1990. This company has now been taken over by Arriva.

Above: In the market town of Barcelos in May 1990, a smart 1970 AEC Reliance 6U3ZL with two-door J Martins body in the fleet of Costa e Colino, no.91 (SO-92-07), with an imported, recently purchased MAN SL200 (no.109, QT-62-00) of the same fleet in the background.

the former Rodoviária de Lisboa was privatised. It successfully operates 120 buses on over 60 routes around Cascais, Estoril and Oeiras. A massive fleet

Left: *Getting by with a little help from Mafrense – dwarfed by the vast Palácio de Mafra in its hometown, Mafrense no.68 (AO-39-23), a 1973 UTIC-AEC U2047 with UTIC bodywork, seen in September 1988 about to depart for the seaside village of Ericeira.*

Below: *In the centre of Estoril in September 1991, RN no.CS826 (DN-45-88), a 1973 UTIC-AEC U2055 with UTIC body. This part of the nationalised RN company is now Stagecoach Portugal.*

replacement brought 60 Marcopolo-bodied Scanias into the fleet after Stagecoach took over, and these have been joined more recently by Camo-bodied Dennis Dart SLFs. The UK influence has recognised the potential for developing more leisure travel, and an attractive multi-lingual booklet suggests round trips using service buses, and makes it easy by offering day rover and weekly network tickets. The booklet even includes timetables, information that seemed to be treated as a state secret in RN days.

There are two Routemasters used on hop-on/hop-off services linking Estoril and Cascais with the beaches to the west, and the quaint hilltop town of Sintra. There – or at least near there – you'll find the historic Sintra-Atlântico Tramway. Opened in 1904 to link Sintra with the Atlantic coast at Praia das Maçãs, I found it almost by mistake in 1985 when it was a forgotten outpost of RN. Then it was running only from Banzão to the beach, and some summers it never ran at all. Stagecoach inherited the tramway and set about negotiating with Sintra council to reopen the tramway towards the town, terminating

Above: *Outside the Palácio Nacional de Sintra in September 1991, a 1982 Leyland/UTIC Europa – rear-engined Tiger integral – on sightseeing work, RN no.L383 (AI-07-79).*

Left: *Splendidly converted for upmarket open-top tours on the Estoril Coast in 1987, this RN Leyland Atlantean Special, no.CS895 (EF-49-26) started life in 1968 as a UTIC-bodied bus with the independent Transul, running services across the Tagus bridge from Lisbon, before being absorbed into RN.*

at Ribeira de Sintra. This has happened, and there are still plans to extend the line back into Sintra station, which would greatly improve its tourist appeal. Stagecoach is no longer involved in the operation, but the Sintra Tramway is well worth a visit.

If this sounds like a plug for Portuguese tourism, well maybe it is. Portugal is a delightful country, with an attractive climate and a lot to see – and that includes the buses, of course. There are probably fewer attractions for diehard UK busfans looking for reminders of the way things were, but there is more than enough to make up for the lack of AECs.

And there are still the memories and the photos of the earlier trips – and the Metosul Atlanteans, of course. And if you ever find Aluguer – let me know. **CB**

PORTFOLIO

In the first of two Portfolio features we show the work of ROBIN HANNAY

Left: *Robin Hannay's 1960s colour photos feature secondhand acquisitions by fleets, some of which rarely bought other than new buses. Decidedly unusual in Midland Red colours is this 1949 Guy Arab III with Barnard 35-seat body, one of two new to Kemp & Shaw and acquired by Midland Red with that business. No.4843 (FJF 90) at Lichfield in the autumn of 1962.*
All photos by Robin Hannay

Below: *The first dual-purpose Yeates Pegasus body, on a Bedford SB chassis reworked to give a front entrance, 951 UVT, was purchased by Becketts of Bucknall and ended up in the Potteries fleet, as seen here at Cheadle in 1964.*

Above: *Seen at Shanklin working for Southern Vectis in August 1966, this ex-Hants & Dorset 1944 Bristol K5G, no.909 (FRU 303), has an older Strachans body extensively rebuilt by Hants & Dorset.*

Below: *Walsall Corporation bought trolleybuses from several fleets, This is one of eight Weymann-bodied Sunbeam Ws bought in 1959 when they were 11 years old from Maidstone & District – they had previously worked in the Hastings Tramways fleet. They gave Walsall (and its successor West Midlands PTE) a further 11 years service. No.309 (BDY 816) is seen in June 1968.*

Above: *A most unusual vehicle to find in a municipal fleet – a Dennis Lancet UF with centre entrance Plaxton Venturer body bought by Darwen Corporation in 1960, when XNU 140 was five years old.*

Left: *To deal with a shortage of buses when new deliveries were delayed, Halifax bought five 16-year old Roe-bodied AEC Regent III from Leeds City Transport, two going to the Corporation fleet and the others to the JOC fleet. They were not repainted during their Halifax service.*

Above: *Exhibited at the 1954 Commercial Motor Show, this ex-Maidstone & District AEC Reliance/ Harrington, TKM 304, was bought by Yorkshire Woollen in 1968 as a short-term measure.*

Left: *An unusual model to find in any large fleet – apart of course from Aldershot & District – this Dennis Lancet 3 J10 with Associated Coachbuilders 39-seat body was new in February 1951 to J Hurst and was acquired by Northern General with that business a few months later. It is seen in Newcastle as Northern no.1456 (MPT 632).*

PORTFOLIO

Edinburgh buses in the 1960s and early 1970s photographed by IAIN MacGREGOR

Above: *A little editorial indulgence here in the choice of eight of Iain MacGregor's Edinburgh Corporation photographs. Iain started taking good colour photos in the early 1960s, before many other enthusiasts, and has supplied photos for many magazines and books. The first photo, taken in September 1961, shows no.386 (DWS 128), an Edinburgh Corporation (ECT) 1943 Guy Arab I with its 1949 Northern Counties bodywork, in Princes Street. These buses lasted a further year in ECT service.*
All photos by Iain MacGregor

Left: *The mainstay of the ECT postwar bus fleet until the mid-1950s were the 72 Daimlers with Birmingham-style Metro-Cammell bodies. Ten were CVD6 model with Daimler CD6 engines and the rest, like no. 139 (GSF 970) of 1949, were CVG6 with Gardner 6LW engines. No.139 is seen in North St Andrew Street in June 1963, about to pass Edinburgh's bus station.*

Left: *Your editor's all-time favourite buses were ECT's 21 all-Leyland Titan PD2/12s, bought in 1952, particularly in their original form, as shown. No.249 (JWS 69) climbs the Mound in September 1961. These buses were modernised in 1961-3 with Leyland-style glassfibre fronts and lasted with ECT until 1970.*

Below: *ECT's most famous Leyland double-deckers were probably the 'monstrous masses of shivering tin', the 300 Metro-Cammell Orion-bodied lightweight Titan PD2/20s bought to replace Edinburgh's trams in 1954-7. No.741 (NSF 741) is seen in March 1969 on the last stage of its journey to suburban Colinton. In spite of concerns about their robustness, these buses had long lives; no.741 was withdrawn in 1976 after 20 years' service.*

Right: *Seventy Guy Arab IV with Alexander bodies were bought in 1955/6 to assist with the final stages of the tram-bus conversion programme. No.960 (OFS 960) is seen in March 1969 on an enthusiasts' trip, at Clerwood terminus. These buses had all been withdrawn by 1972.*

Below: *Before it took the plunge and switched to Atlanteans, ECT bought two batches of forward entrance Alexander-bodied Leyland Titan PD3s. Brand-new no.658 (ASC 658B), a PD3/6 (with ECT-fitted glassfibre front end) is seen in July 1964 at Portobello Town Hall on the busy cross-city 26 service.*

Above: *When they were available, Edinburgh buses were popular secondhand purchases. The former ECT no.440 (LFS 440), one of the first, 1954, batch of MCCW Orion-bodied Leyland PD2/20s, is caught in Saltcoats in June 1971 in service with A1 Service co-operative member A Hunter (no.16), now with platform doors.*

Left: *Another A1 Service member, T Hunter, bought two of the ECT 1956 Guy Arab IV/Alexander in 1970, again fitting them with platform doors. NSF 902 is seen in Saltcoats in February 1970.*

SUDBURY SCENE IN THE SIXTIES

GEOFF MILLS takes us back to 1960s Suffolk

J Amos & Son, Belchamp St Paul, Essex (still extant) served Sudbury on Wednesdays, Thursdays and Sundays from Ovington. Its all-Bedford fleet of three (livery red/cream) comprised an OWB/Duple (JVX 307 seen in Market Hill on 9 November 1961), an OB/Thurgood and an OB/Strachan.
All photos by Geoff Mills

A S A SCHOOLBOY, cycle rides to Sudbury, Suffolk – only 15 miles from my Essex home – were well within scope to view an array of independents that descended on the town, particularly on Thursdays, market day. The acquisition of a motorcycle and 35mm camera financed by a meagre apprentice draughtsman's pay allowed more frequent visits and better-quality photographs – although financial constraints stopped the 'shoot at every psv in sight' policy. Most operators that served the town owned an example of the ubiquitous Bedford OB, so the less prolific types – particularly heavyweight chassis, very much in the minority then, plus double-deckers, were the popular targets.

Unfortunately, Corona Coaches Ltd went into liquidation in 1959 and an interesting fleet of vehicles disappeared from Market Hill. The take-over of Longs of Glemsford in the August of the previous year had introduced double-deckers to the distinctive chocolate/tangerine livery. However Corona's failure gave impetus to other established operators – like Letch, Rule and Theobald. The latter introduced double-deckers into a Bedford-biased fleet.

Sudbury lost Corona but gained Mulleys Motorways of Ixworth operating out of the Acton depot, providing a long-established London service and introducing a town service. Thus on Thursdays, the town's market day, no fewer than ten operators would appear on Market Hill during the early 1960s. A selection of the rolling stock in use in that fascinating period is illustrated. **CB**

Above: *H C Chambers & Son Ltd, Bures, Suffolk (still extant) served Sudbury on Colchester-Bury St Edmunds route on weekdays (not Sundays) and to Haverhill via Halstead on Fridays. Its fleet of 12 (livery red/cream/black) comprised seven Bedfords (three OB/Duple, three SB/Duple and one SB/Yeates) and five Guy Arabs, one each with Crossley, East Lancs and Roe bodies, and HWO 341, seen on 9 December 1967 at Market Hill, an ex-Red & White example, one of two with Duple bodies.*

Below: *H S Springett, t/a Jennings, Ashen, Essex, served Sudbury from Ashen on Thursdays. Its fleet of seven (livery duo-green) comprised two Bedford OB/Duple, two Bedford SB/Duple, one AEC Reliance/Duple and two Leyland-MCW Olympics, one of which, ex-demonstrator KOC 233, is seen on 26 March 1964 homeward-bound from Sudbury; it was an HR40 model, acquired by Jennings in 1951 and withdrawn in 1972. The company sold out to Hedingham & District in 1984.*

11.23 sees two Northerns going out on frequent services. One's a Dawdon 23 with yet another NCB Guy – but look, the other's a Pennywell 74 which has a heavyweight 1952 Guy working it and ignoring its additional six inches of width, d'you notice the London RT-like proportions of the body? That's because it's a Park Royal product and like all Northern group double-deck bodies built on new chassis after 1951, it's metal-framed. Ah, now the 11.25 departures are starting and one of the three Northerns coming out at this end is a decker with platform doors, a Met-Cam Orion-bodied Guy on a Durham 57. The second bus is a 1956 medium-weight Park Royal-bodied Guy Arab pointing itself to Newcastle on the 40. I'm sure you'll have noticed some resemblance to that other exciting London idea, the new Routemaster, in this design of body which you'll probably agree would beat the Orion in any bus beauty contest. Next comes yet another all-Leyland PD2/3 doing a 'Shields 14, this one from Easington Lane, and finally on the other side another SDO Weymann Tiger Cub beginning to make Its way to New Silksworth on one of service 50's prongs. Now at 11.28 the other blue unrebodied utility Guy leaves for New Silksworth on the shorter 51.

11.30's just about to come up and d'you see that odd-looking Northern saloon there, with the driver just climbing into the cab? Well, that's a 'loaf tin', one of the famous 1951/3 AEC-NGT rebuilds, a 30ft-long 43-seater created from a prewar 27ft 6in-long Regal. It's going to Hebburn on the half-past eleven service 9D which runs hourly and omits the Tyne Tunnel. You'll notice that the driving position is further forward than normal, as with the Brush Guy saloons. In fact this one's the prototype and with two locally-based 'production models' it works hard between Wear and Tyne. That Guy saloon we saw earlier deputises if a loaf tin is unavailable. The body's timber-framed but can you name its builder? I'm not surprised if you can't. It's Picktree of Chester-le-Street. They're no longer engaged in PSV work but they did a fair amount for Northern during 1950-4, some of it rebodying. Yeah, that deeply-arched roof line evokes memories of prewar BMMOs (locally known as 'aad Sosses'), and we used to have plenty of those in the Northern fleet. Oh, the loaf tin's rough old 7.7-litre engine and screaming crash-box provide a symphony of aural delights – in fact, the best there is now that there are no more prewar Leylands hereabouts.

Stylish

Anyway, here come three more Northern half past elevens: a stylish-looking Northern Burlingham-

In the early to mid-1950s search for economy through lighter weight, several manufacturers produced integral vehicles, that is, without a separate chassis. An example was coachbuilder Beadle of Dartford which marketed luxury coach and service bus applications of light alloy construction using mechanical units produced by Commer of Luton, an associate within what was then the Rootes Group, although production was short-lived. Northern, already operating 25 AEC-Park Royal Monocoach integral buses new in 1954, acquired two Beadle service saloons in 1955 of which the second, no.1626, is shown here pausing at Chester-le-Street. The pair would be withdrawn as early as 1959.
A B Cross

bodied AEC Reliance, new this year, on a Consett 5, another Brush-bodied Guy decker on a Red House 6B and see, one more Guy – but go on, look at its body and now guess that make! Ah no, d'you see, it isn't ECW: it's NCB and metal-framed, to the final design of the builder before the firm's demise in 1950. You may be forgiven the mistake, because due to personnel movement it's purely of ECW early postwar proportions, other than for being 8ft wide. This one's on service 48 and going to all the way to North Hylton which is just a three-minute run beyond Castletown. At the other end there goes another 1956 Northern Park Royal-bodied Guy on the 11.30 'West' 40, running through from Newcastle and d'you notice, yet another DDS delight on the Darlington D7: a 1947 ex-ABC Leyland Tiger PS1 carrying a 1950 Willowbrook body that came off a 1946 ex-ABC Dennis Lancet earlier this year but was fitted until 1955 to a 1937 United AEC Regal, replacing that one's original Brush coach body! (are you still with me?) The Leyland and Dennis originally had Raine bodies, built in Spennymoor.

Three more deckers leave now, for 11.32 sees a Northern Met-Cam Orion Guy venturing out on a Newcastle 22, another gorgeous SDO Regent away on a 14 to South Hetton – that's six minutes beyond Easington Lane via Hazard Lane, and a similar bus but with Leyland PD2/1 chassis in line astern on the Durham 57. Next, out on time at 11.33 are the Pennywell 74 being worked by another Brush Guy decker and the Parkside 77 with one of the usual

In 1951/3, Northern rebuilt what were originally 12 prewar AEC Regal chassis and lengthened them from 27ft 6in to 30ft for fitting with new Picktree 43-seat bodywork. With 7.7-litre engine and crash gearbox they were delectably raucous, although hardly handsome. Nevertheless, they provided a relatively cheap and light alternative to first-generation underfloor-engined buses of similar seating capacity which tended to be heavy in price, weight and running costs, and of which Northern bought none. No.1478 is seen here in Newcastle but three others ran on the Sunderland - Jarrow services until 1959 when it became possible to use double-deckers.
J Fozard

older NCB Guys . . . and that's another similar bus heading south on the 11.35 service 5C to Deneside Mission, six miles away. A couple of SDO Leylands are chasing it for part of the way, a Saro Tiger Cub and a PD1, on a New Silksworth 50 and a Hollycarrside 41 respectively. Ho-ho, you've remembered, the second one's the bus we saw on the same service half-an-hour ago. Leaving at the same time northbound we see yet another superb SDO Regent doing a 'Shields 14 from South Hetton and one more Met-Cam Orion Guy doing a Newcastle 40. And now, at 11.36 and nearly up the staircase of the Newcastle bus is the Northern Guy on hire to SDO that was on the 11.04 New Silksworth 51.

Oh that's true, other than for the A690 Durham road and the A693 west of Chester-le-Street, most of the highways used by these buses have little more

A five-cylinder tough Guy – Northern General no.1407 of 1952, with good-looking Park Royal bodywork showing an obvious similarity to the London RT-family design. Seen before delivery and initially to be allocated to Sunderland depot, it displays an unladen weight of 8.1.0 although a few others in the batch of 20 stated 8.4.0. Anything considerably more than 7¹/2 tons was a struggle for the Gardner 5LW. Note the lining out, black edging and the then recently-introduced smaller-sized fleet name. The number blind settings are not authentic.
David Wayman collection

than moderate gradients of no great length. Those to Tyneside destinations have several relatively low-lying stretches that are practically flat, although buses on the 64 to Newcastle do climb for some three miles from an altitude of 160ft at Washington to 533ft beyond Wrekenton, before a dramatic two-mile descent through Gateshead to less than 100ft at the Tyne Bridge. That road to Durham, though, has a few surprises. From 120ft here, it rises overall to 370ft in the five miles to Stoneygate and soon after that plunges through Houghton Cut on a half-mile drop to 210ft with a stretch at 1 in 8 near the top. Then after climbing gradually again over six miles to 300ft, it descends to 100ft on 1 in 9 and then 1 in 12 during the last mile to Durham Market Place. When those five-cylinder Guy eight-tonners were on the 57 regularly, heading in this direction well-laden they sometimes had snails overtaking them!

Dive-bomber

Good heavens, is it 11.40 already? Well, that's the cue for another BL-class United Lodekka to leave on a 'Bishop' 57 as the older Northern NCB Guy to our left gets ready for the 11.41 Thornley 21. We've two going out at 42-past: another SDO Regent on the Easington Lane 14 and a United BBL on the 'West'

40. Oh but look, that saloon sounding like a dive-bomber is an oddity! We hadn't noticed it creeping in behind another bus and now it's making for Consett on the 11.43 number 4 via Number One, the hourly deviation I mentioned earlier. Tee-hee, I'm not surprised you can't identify it, because it's an integrally-built Beadle-Commer with raucous Commer TS3 two-stroke engine which should give good fuel returns. There are two of them, the lightest underfloor-engined saloons in the fleet, new in 1955 and right outside the mainstream of BET vehicle policy. Obviously Northern's seeing how they compare with other types. They do struggle a bit on some of those climbs up to Consett. See, another

Somewhat more comfortable than its Northern Orion Guy neighbours, SDO's well-filled no.274, a 1955 Metro-Cammell Orion-bodied Leyland Titan PD2/12, is about to set off southbound from Park Lane bus station. The building behind the bus is the Northern company's office and canteen block.
David Wayman collection

heavyweight Park Royal Guy on the 74 follows, conveying some of Pennywell's 10,000 residents (although the Corporation carries many more passengers on its own two services to Pennywell, not touching Park Lane). Yes, we saw that unrebodied SDO wartime Guy 32 minutes ago, too, and now it's doing another New Silksworth 51, the 11.44.

Aha, now the town hall ding-dongs announce the quarter hour and we've more Northern synchronised action. The Weymann Orion Guy leaving as the 11.45 Red House 6A is the one we saw on the 11.03 Pennywell 74. An Arab of the same pack continues to 'Shields from Easington Lane on the 14 but close behind it on the Newcastle 40 through from 'West' – behold the ultimate in Northern double-deck comfort, providing you're not too long-legged and can put up with the rattling of the sliding vents (and 32 miles or 120 minutes of rattles!). Yes, for that Park Royal-bodied Leyland Titan – one of ten new last year – is a PD2/12 with platform doors. But seriously, if you really want comfortable seats you'll have to travel in a heavyweight Park Royal or Weymann Guy decker, although even these are surpassed by the superb torso-huggers in both types of Royal Tiger. Oh and look, that SDO bus on a Houghton 50 is another Weymann Tiger Cub.

You'll have noticed that sometimes between the multiples of five past the hour there's a lull in departures and then several at once, such as now. Between 11.45 and 11.50 there's only one movement

out and it's the 11.47 Durham 57 which a platform-doored Orion Guy of Northern's is working. Now coming by us at 11.50 we've a Monocoach on the 15 to Consett and another loaf tin leaving on the 'forked' 26 route on which this journey by-passes the Tyne Tunnel in favour of Hebburn (Monkton Lane Estate). Maybe I should mention also that the two 26s and one 9D per hour, while they have three different routeings beyond Jarrow town centre, give a co-ordinated 20-minute frequency between here and Jarrow (Prince Consort Terrace). From noon until seven o'clock this evening there'll be short-workings on service 26 to Boldon Colliery, usually with deckers, twice an hour. What's on the other side? Oh, leaving for Darlington on the D3 there's a machine with an interesting history, although that's not unusual in the DDS fleet: it's a DB-class 1938 ex-United Bristol L5G with 1949 ECW body transferred from a prewar Leyland Tiger TS7 two years ago. Great! And it's being followed by a Northern Met-Cam Orion Guy with platform doors on a Newcastle-'West' 40, itself just ahead of the navy blue PD1 we saw on its previous trip to Hollycarrside as a 41 half an hour ago.

Encore

Blue is the colour again now at 11.52 as one more handsome, harmonious SDO Regent performs music on its way to South Hetton on the 14, and the rebodied wartime Guy that was on the 11.20 New Silksworth 51 gives an encore. Ah, but now guess what Northern type's getting ready for the 11.53 Parkside 77? OK, no prizes, it's an older NCB Guy. There's also an 11.53 Pennywell 74 and this other similar bus working it is the one that went out as the eleven o'clock Red House 6B.

So now we're about to spot the rash of 11.55 departures and oh, we've got the blues again for there's yet a further delectable SDO Regent on this South Shields 14 from South Hetton and an Orion Leyland PD2/12 on the 57 to Durham. Now we're seeing red as a heavyweight Weymann Guy sallies forth on the 'long' route to Newcastle, 64, taking 57 minutes. This compares with 51 on service 22 with which it's co-ordinated as far as Washington, and 45 minutes on the direct number 40 on which this 1956 Park Royal Arab's just pulling out as a guy leaps aboard. Hard on its heels is the SDO Weymann-bodied Tiger Cub that previously worked the 11.05 New Silksworth 50, doing the same once more.

And now at 11.57, drawing away to go south we see a United BBL again, this one going beyond 'West' on the hourly Middlesbrough 40. It'll take it two hours, 14 minutes to cover the 35 miles. That would

Part of the Leyland empire since 1951, Albion produced during 1957-60 a lightened version of the lightweight Leyland Tiger Cub called the Aberdonian, powered by the 5.76-litre Leyland O.350 engine. Northern took five with Weymann Hermes bodywork in 1957 and here no.1758, with no.1757 behind and amid the smiles of enthusiasts, catches the sunshine at Newcastle's Marlborough Crescent bus station when new.
A B Cross

be a pleasant enough journey for hobbyists like us but for the earnest traveller Durham District's D1 and D2 are shorter, and quicker by 34 and 24 minutes respectively to the same place.

Right, midday's almost upon us and the town hall clock will be bracing itself for the proclamation. The smart saloons of the Economic Bus Service which go to South Shields by two coastal routes have run past us at intervals but as their terminus is at the far end of the lane we've paid no attention to them. Elsewhere, not using the bus station, we'll see Northern buses on other services operated jointly with the corporation and with SDO, and SDO buses on their own local. In fact we've noticed some of them turning briefly into and out of yon end of the lane, weaving westward on their journeys. But we said we'd only an hour so let's spring out of Park Lane before we start drooling over the 12.00 departures . . . **CB**

CHRIS DREW tells the story of Green Line double-deckers, illustrated with his own drawings

THE YEAR WAS 1931. 'Green Line Coaches Ltd.' had been registered on 9 July the year previously as the coach-operating arm of the London General Omnibus Co. Already it had begun to sweep away other small operators and was now trying to mould the whole outfit into a fully integrated working unit. New, luxurious coaches were arriving and passengers were being wooed on to them. Order was being created out of chaos.

The time, late autumn. The place, a country bus stop just this side of Reigate. A passenger waits with his collar turned against the first chill September wind. He is waiting for his Green Line up to town. Into sight comes not his usual fare, but a stately green galleon of a double-decker in full sail. This may be rather a romantic view of the proceedings, but I guess it must have been a surprise!

LT1137 (GP 3456) was Green Line's first foray into giving passengers unsurpassed views of the countryside, ie a double-decker. The chassis used was a long-wheelbase AEC Renown from a batch of single-deckers being produced at the time. As such, it was to remain unique. The power unit was the same 110mm bore petrol engine as used in the 'Scooters' but I have seen it written that at some time in its life it was fitted with a General Motors two-stroke engine for an experimental period – but I know no more.

The bodywork was built at Chiswick and nowadays would be called a concept design. The most noticeable feature was the elegant concave curve at the front, which travelled from waistline to roof. As built it had an open front entrance but this was soon altered and a sliding door was fitted. This was more becoming the quiet, warm, luxury interior that was to be expected of such a service. Although the entrance was at the front, the staircase was at the rear. Odd you might say, but I think it was so that the maximum number of passengers would have an uninterrupted view forward. Mind you, it would have meant quite a jog to get to those elusive front seats upstairs. To keep within the legal length the rear overhang was reduced, giving a bobtail look. To combat this, window bays were wider, giving a more sleek appearance. Inside, LT1137 had just 50 comfortable seats plus one last surprise, a sunshine roof, which could be opened on the more pleasant of days although, I would have thought that overhanging trees might have been a problem.

In September 1931, LT1137 was set to work on route 'E' running between Reigate and Bushey. She worked

LT1137

Q188

electronically-operated epicyclic gearbox. It carried a distinctive 51-seat Park Royal body with a sliding door just behind the front axle. When the door was open it disappeared between the two skins of the bodywork. The lack of a radiator at the front meant that the stylists at PRV could produce a sinuous curve from ground to roof which was similar to another vehicle that was going to appear several years later, the RT.

The windows upstairs were designed to look twice their length, with a slender chrome pillar where the middle bay should have been. The effect was one of being long, slim and a bit racy. However this was not carried on downstairs except for the rearmost bay but even so, with rounded window corners the consequence was very pleasant. The whole package was wrapped up in a very fine two-tone green livery capped off with a silver roof. The style of three-piece blind was unusual – a main number/via box with an ultimate box underneath and a similar one above set to carry the Green Line

on Green Line duties for a creditable four years before being downgraded to a bus, upseated to 56, door removed and stairs relocated to the front and sent to Hatfield garage. It settled into country bus life and stayed that way until 1942 when it was withdrawn to save fuel. Somehow it found its way to Hounslow garage where it was to end its days, in the back, out of sight until it was scrapped in 1946.

Second try

Green Line's first attempt could have been thought of as a passable success but its second try was far from. In 1935, authority was gained to produce a prototype double-deck coach for use on the Romford services. The eventual outcome was Q188.

The 'Q' was AEC's revolutionary side-engined chassis built between 1932-6. General at first, then London Transport were smitten by the type and 238 examples were taken into stock, both as buses and coaches. Included in these numbers were five double-deckers and one of these was a three-axle version, (again a single-deck type), which was to become Q188.

Q188 had the then standard 7.7-litre petrol engine and fluid flywheel transmission. According to some sources, it also had an

RT97 on the 721

name. As with LT1137 the seating was well-spaced and very comfortable although the inward-facing seats were not really suitable for longer distances.

Q188 was finally taken into stock early in 1937 but hung around until the middle of 1938 by which time the idea of using it on the on the Romford road had gone to the wall. It was registered DGO 500 and with indecent haste it was stripped of its Green Line status and sent to Hertford garage to join the other double-deck Qs to work on the route 310. It spent its short working life at this garage, that life ending in the early war years.

Pay-as-you-enter

Before the war, London Transport had been dabbling with 'pay-as-you-enter' on double-deckers using two trolleybuses and also two STLs. This was not as we know it now, but it meant paying the conductor who sat behind a cash till from where he issued tickets.

In July 1944, RT97 was damaged when it was caught in an air-raid. Initially sent to Birmingham for repair in the corporation workshops, it was brought back before any work was started. It had been chosen for another PAYE experiment. Chiswick rebuilt the bus adding rear doors (quite rare in London at the time) and moving the staircase one bay forward to give the largest platform area possible. Two emergency exits were added, one in the rear wall, shaped like the one upstairs, and a door type opposite the entrance. The seating was reduced to 50. The conversion was completed in December 1945. It was sent to work at the beginning of the following January. RT97 arrived at Kingston ready to join the two PAYE STLs on the 65 route. You may have guessed by now that RT97 was still red but this was not to last much longer. As with the experimental STLs, passengers didn't take to well to PAYE on RT97. If there were to many people waiting at the stop to get on the platform, the driver just had to hold on until the conductor could take enough fares to get the passengers off the kerb – an everyday scene nowadays! Anyway, that might be all right on a sunny day but when the weather was inclement, the complaints came thick and fast. Timetables went out the window and the older STs, the staple diet on the 65, were running rings around all the PAYE buses. RT97 lasted less than three months on the 65 and on 25 March 1946, it was sent back to Chiswick.

It was presumed that if RT97 was used on a less densely-populated route, it still might work. To this end, it was painted into Green Line's two-tone green livery and made ready for work, which it was by 18 April. One minor modification was added. This was a sliding window behind the conductor's seat. This done, it was sent to Romford (yes, again). It was

RTC1

set to work on the 721 alongside utility Daimlers. Compared with the aforementioned, RT97 must have been like a little touch of heaven. Although the PAYE system worked better in this sphere of operation, it was still slow to load and there really was no reason for a conductor to be seated when there was plenty of time to collect fares in the time-honoured fashion. RT97 remained in service until January 1947 when it was withdrawn and sent back to head office to await its fate.

Butterfly

RT97 went into Chiswick a caterpillar and reappeared two years later as a butterfly. Both the body and chassis were completely taken apart and what was in essence a new vehicle was to take shape. Work started in June 1948 and by January 1949 it was ready to be shown to the press as RTC1. At first glance, you could see there was an RT in there somewhere, but it was well disguised. First question, where was the radiator? Easy, underneath the stairs. Next! Without that particular lump of iron on the front, the bonnet line was lowered to something reminiscent of the prewar TF class. A toothpaste advert of a grille was laid sideways rounded off with headlights and a chrome strip to hide the joins. The stairs that hid the radiator were moved back to their original position and a door-type emergency exit was located in the back wall. Also under the stairs, connected to the radiator, was a heat exchanger. This used engine coolant to warm the interior on winter days. Nice idea, I hear you say, but all the extra pipework running the length of the bus and back led to problems and, as was to be found out in service, overheating was a major fault.

The body styling was handed over to outside consultants Douglas Scott and Norbert Dutton. A dramatic statement was made by the window design. The effect was one of a continuous sheet of glass from front to back with window size defined by slim aluminium pillars. All four middle bays upstairs and the middle two down, opened to the half way position. The rear doors were kept but the seating was reduced to 46, (26/20). PAYE was thrown out and the conductor took up his/her rightful place making sure that everyone who had their bottoms on the luxury, airline-style seats and were reading their copies of their favourite newspaper by the fluorescent lights paid their way. There was one extra seat. A fold-up type was fitted by the entrance so the conductor had somewhere to mop his/her brow between collecting.

Duple-bodied D145

STL2637

On 31 March, RTC1, still registered FXT 272, was licensed and started a short trial period of Green Line service. At first it was sent to Windsor for no obvious reason because by the 6 April, it was moved to Hertford for the 715. It can't have fitted in anywhere because it moved on to Reigate (711), Hemel Hempstead (708), Windsor again (704) and finally back to Hertford for another spell on the 715. It stayed there from the end of July to November. It was not a success because of the overheating problems mentioned earlier. Trying to recoup something for all the expense, RTC1 was sent south to Leatherhead garage. It was stripped of its Green Line status and put to work on the routes 416 and 468. In March 1952 it was given a light overhaul at which time it lost its comfy seats and fluorescent lighting. RTC1 returned to Leatherhead but only had a short life left. On 1 March 1953, it was finally withdrawn, being uneconomical and unreliable to operate.

Test-bed

It did however have one final job to do at Chiswick. The RTC had grown up in parallel with the Routemaster project and as such proved to be an excellent test-bed for ideas later to appear on that bus. This was to go full circle because of course those features were to appear in the RMCs and RCLs a decade later. It carried on in this guise until March 1955 when it was withdraw for the last time and sold. After passing through several dealers, it ended up as a staff bus for Vernon's Pools in Liverpool. At the end of its time there, RTC1 was due to move to one last owner, Pitbow Ltd of Sandwich in Kent, but it never got there because it was scrapped in Birkenhead in late 1961.

On 31 April 1939 Green Line services were withdrawn in preparation for war. The then-current fleet of Ts and TFs were drafted very quickly into the ambulance service using plans put together at the time of the Munich crisis. Services started again, slowly at first

RT2252 showing blinds for the 726

wartime. The bodywork was built by Duple to a slightly relaxed utility design. The Daimlers were joined in August by five 15STL16s, which were some of the last delivered before the war. These had standard 56-seat LPTB bodies. At first these were used on the summer-only 726 which went from Marylebone to Whipsnade Zoo. Later on, the two classes were thought of as interchangeable.

Livery change

In 1948 a change in livery appeared. The green and white turned to the two-tone green that was to stay with the company into the early 1970s. The STLs were painted for the summer season 726 with the Daimlers having to wait until October when their overhauls started. To cover the loss of the Daimlers, five extra STLs were used. This was all happening about the time London Transport was earmarking later-built STLs for conversion to the ill-fated SRT

but gathered apace, albeit on a much reduced footing. Older vehicles were bought out of retirement to run what little service was left. By winter 1940-1, the burden of trying to maintain an ever-growing service under wartime conditions was taking its toll on vehicles and staff. To help out, about 180 STLs were drafted in to run services. These consisted of central and country buses, front and rear entrance types. As far as I know, none carried Green Line decals. This was only a short respite because shortages of fuel and rubber made it impossible for services to carry on. On 29 September 1942, Green Line services ceased to operate and it was to be that way for the next three-and-a-half years.

Green Line services restarted in February 1946. A month later saw an influx of utility Daimlers. 37 were painted in Green Line livery and set to work from Romford garage for the 721/722 routes, joined in August by five STLs, also repainted correctly. No frills here. No extra comfort. These were ordinary machines just given a makeover. The Daimlers were the CWA6 model, the AEC engine being more acceptable than Daimler's own. They were delivered from November 1945 and held in store at Grays, Epping, Northfleet and Romford garages. Services started on 1 March 1946. 22 vehicles were made ready for the 721 with the rest to be on the road for the 722 by 3 April. The Daimlers can't have been a very comfortable ride, especially on rough roads not repaired from

class. With this in mind, December saw five extra Brush-bodied Daimlers head for Romford to release the STLs for rebuilding.

The Daimlers held sway on the Romford Road for a couple of years, only giving way to new RTs in August 1950. Even then, six were kept to operate the Whipsnade service until October. A few of these also saw service over the Christmas period. They finally left Romford towards the end of

CRL4 before overhaul

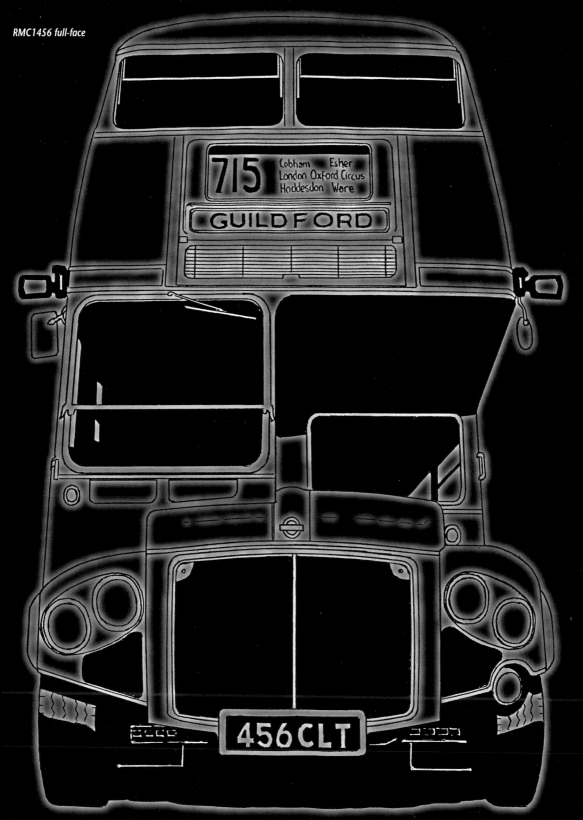

715 Cobham Esher
London Oxford Circus
Hoddesdon Ware

GUILDFORD

456CLT

January 1951. Many went back to central area garages, some still in green livery, later to be repainted red.

Much has been written about the RT over the years so I won't dwell on this type too long. Thirty-six RTs (3224-59) were taken out of the last order delivered in 1950. They were to be used to replace the Daimlers running the Romford Green Line services. Although they were to be operating an upmarket service, they were in fact, little different from the many hundreds ploughing the roads of London and the Home Counties. Only the livery put them apart from the rest. The Lincoln green with light green band, the raised bullseye between decks, the lack of adverts, all gave them an air of superiority. The first batch started work on 1 August and were augmented with batches of 12 in 1952-3, 21 in 1954 and another 16 which were repainted from other liveries in 1960. In theory, this last group were for relief services but this was not always so. In 1965, an order from on high went out to reclassify these RTs as buses. Twenty-three survived these changes. In June 1967, RTs 967, 3606 and 3624 were lost to the cause leaving only 20 but many of these kept their special livery up to and including 1969 even if they were operating ordinary routes because they had been replaced by Routemasters in the mid-1960s.

Routemaster prototype

In the late 1950s London Transport was ready to put the Routemaster out on trial. In the light of increasing passenger traffic on some Green Line routes it came as no surprise when one of the four Routemaster prototypes was fitted out to coach standards. CRL4, as it was first known, pulled together all the knowledge gained over the previous 15 years – higher road speed, more comfort for the passengers and driver, rear doors for heat conservation, better suspension and all-round smoother riding qualities. At first seating 55 (later 57), the Eastern Coach Works body was a step up in standards for the travelling public used to a draughty RT. As with so many Green Line double-deckers, CRL4, (SLT 59) was put to work, in October 1957, on the Romford Road which by that time was nothing more than a slightly extended bus route for which the CRL was over-

specified. One can reason, I suppose, that working alongside the RTs, it wouldn't get noticed and a direct comparison could be made. After a couple of months on the 721, CRL4 was removed and sent to High Wycombe for driver training. It was then transferred to Reigate for the 711 route on which it duly started on 8 January 1958. Passenger comments were favourable but the drivers were not so happy. A vibration problem in the front bulkhead made driving long distances uncomfortable, so action was taken to rectify this. Later, in May of 1958, CRL4 was taken into Chiswick to have its rear suspension changed from coil to air. Air suspension did give a softer, sometimes spongy, ride but it was kept and indeed this type of cushioning was installed in some later versions. In July, it was put back into service from Tunbridge Wells on the 704. This allowed for monitoring of the new suspension under high road speeds.

In the following years it moved around to other garages for service on the 715, 718 and 716 with odd visits to Chiswick to strengthen sub-frames. In April 1962 it was reclassified RMC4 as a precursor to the new batch of Routemaster coaches arriving later that year. It was allocated to Hertford garage ready to join the coming RMCs. Between April and December 1964, RMC4 received a long drawn-out overhaul at which time it acquired a standard RMC bonnet but managed to keep its unique, (for an RMC), three-piece blind.

After the experimental years with RMC4 proved satisfactory, an order

RMC1461 rear view

RCL2260 on the 715

to many people was a retrograde step. Along with other minor but noticeable body changes and the application of adverts, albeit only below the rear platform window, the sparkle was lost and by the time the Country Area/Green Line services were passed to the NBC at the end of 1969, they were looking a little the worse for wear.

Wrong time

By the mid-1960s, the heyday of the Green Line under LT ownership was over. Expansion of the Underground, electrification of BR lines meant quicker journeys into town without traffic jams. Into this world was born the last Green Line double-decker of the LT dynasty, the RCL. It was the right bus but at totally the wrong time. These wonderful buses were built to the maximum 30ft length, pulled along by the larger AV691 11.3-litre engine. It had 65 well-spaced seats and all the body modifications built in, not added.

On 2 June 1965 they entered service along the Romford Road again, turning full circle. Twenty years earlier, the Daimlers saw the expansion of the east London services while the RCLs were to see their decline. The image of Green Line coaches was getting dated even with the injection of the RCLs and by the time all was handed over to the NBC the service was nearly lost. Both the RMCs and RCLs went on to operate as very comfortable if underseated buses for London Country and even later back with London Transport – shades of older times when coaches were downgraded to country buses then to red buses. The NBC did go on to try double-deckers on some revamped Green Line services but that falls outside the remit of this article.

Over the years, many other double-deckers have worked on Green Line services as reliefs. I've seen RTs, red and green, RMs, RMLs red and green. Back in the Coronation year, almost everything that could be used, was.

In my mind, I still think nothing could be quite the same as sitting upstairs at the front of an RMC, windows wound down and the Surrey countryside flashing by in a blur as my 'Stately Galleon' ruled the road home. **CB**

for 68 similar vehicles was placed. These were to have Park Royal bodywork, the norm, and AEC running units as opposed to the Leyland ones used by RMC4. The bodyshell was basically the same as the central area buses but it was tweaked with platform doors, 57 comfy seats, twin headlights, higher road speed, two-piece blinds and a livery to turn heads. Delivery started in June 1962. By August, 20 were available, (12 at Hertford and eight at Guildford) so that by the 29th the 715 and 715A could be converted in one fell swoop. In the next few months RMCs spread over many more routes. I came on to the enthusiast scene at about this time. I lived near Roehampton in south-west London and I remember RMCs all over the place – 715, 716 and 716A in Barnes and the 718 in Putney. I can still recall the pleasure of riding the 715 to Guildford to see relatives. The fast run round the Kingston bypass left an impression on me, but I suppose that could have been the indifferent road surface (concrete slab and pitch) which made a noise similar to a railway carriage going over rail joints.

After only a few years in service, livery changes were in the air. The first step was to remove the metal bullseye from between the decks to be replaced by a larger transfer set further forward. The underlined Green Line name was replaced by one with equal-sized letters. Later the pale green window surrounds were painted the main body colour. This,

No3: Walsall Corporation Transport

Born: 1904
Died: October 1969

How did it begin? As a tram operator. It bought the South Staffordshire Tramways company from BET in 1901 and ran it as a lessee for three years before taking full control. As the late Reg Wilson noted in his 'Municipal Buses' book in 1997, it bought its first buses in 1915 and began replacing trams with buses in 1925; between 1931 and 1933 it replaced the rest of them with trolleybuses.

Were these decorated like the trams? Not in the same colours. Walsall's wore the same brown or maroon and cream as BET's other Black Country fleets, but it painted its buses blue and cream from the outset. The shades of blue changed at times over the years, as did the proportions and shades of relief colours, but the overall theme of blue remained right up to – and beyond – acquisition by the new West Midlands PTE in 1969. In the earlier days, Walsall also was one of the places to incorporate something more of the technology of the bus in its title, adopting the fleetname Walsall Corporation Motors for a time.

What made it so special? Perhaps you should be asking who made it so special.

All right, then, who? Ronald Edgley Cox, the Yorkshire-born general manager who ran the undertaking for its last 17 years. Edgley Cox was a man whose innovative ideas set Walsall's buses far apart from those run in most other fleets. His specifications ensured that this relatively small West Midlands town's buses were frequently the talking points at Commercial Motor Show exhibitions up to the year before WMPTE took over.

What made them so unusual? He thought beyond the box that confined most operators' thinking, was prepared to buy early examples of many manufacturers' new models and to go farther by commissioning his own unusual versions.

Go on: He bought early examples of the AEC Bridgemaster, Dennis Loline and Leyland Atlantean, bought half a dozen Bedford SB buses when most municipal managers would have run a mile from the very idea of mass-produced lightweights and he snapped up some surplus RTLs from London Transport when they first came on the market in 1959. But that was tame.

What was wild, then? Persuading the Ministry of Transport in 1954 to let him run a batch 22 Sunbeam F4A four-wheel 30ft trolleybuses when the rest of the country was still compelled to run six-wheelers for anything over 27ft long, and doing the wackiest of things with the Daimler Fleetline.

How wacky? When everyone else took the standard 30ft product with its entrance ahead of the front axle, he persuaded the engineers in Coventry to build him a short wheelbase 25ft 7in model in 1962 with no overhang and a sliding door behind the front axle. He thought it would be more manœuvrable. And he must have known it would look more like a trolleybus. It was followed by 54 slightly longer wheelbase versions with a short front overhang; the last 25 came with a narrow entrance ahead of the front axle and the others got one later to make them suitable for driver-only operation. But there was an equally wacky Fleetline of quite different dimensions.

How equally wacky? This was the only UK example of a CR36, principally a 36ft South African market model with an offside rear Cummins V6 engine. Walsall had it bodied by Northern Counties, which had built the short Fleetlines and was more open to non-standard bodywork than most of its competitors. It had 86 seats, a front and rear staircase, a front and rear door and closed circuit television to help the driver control what was going on 34ft behind him. It doesn't seem to have been much of a success and was sold before its natural time, but it was one heck of a way to remember Walsall Corporation.

Alan Millar

Walsall's 1954 batch of 30ft two-axle Sunbeam F4A/Willowbrooks paved the way for universal use of the 30ft two-axle double-decker two years later.
Michael Dryhurst

FOUR-BAY WATCH

MICHAEL DRYHURST reveals his obsession with four-bay and five-bay double-deck bodies

FOR THOSE READERS who do not share my fascination with four-bay/five-bay construction, I apologise wholeheartedly for returning to this subject; for those of you who are as four-bay/five-bay intrigued as I am, hopefully here's some more grist for the mill.

The ball was set rolling some four years ago in *Classic Bus* 25, when Geoff Burrows eloquently and expansively set-out to answer a specific point of mine. In 1947, Brighton Corporation took delivery of nos.81-8, and 45-50. The former were AEC Regent III 096l, the latter BUT 9611T; both batches had Weymann bodywork, that on the motorbuses being of four-bay construction while the trolleybus bodies were of five-bay configuration. Why, I asked? And for the answer, turn to page 29 of CB25. However, I think it fair to say that the underlying thrust of

Geoff's article was that the four-bay layout tended to be an AEC by-product, and that four-bay construction double-deckers were more likely to turn-up on chassis manufactured at Southall rather than those built in Bristol, Coventry, Leyland or Wolverhampton, to name but a few. And without in any way wishing to refute Geoff's assertion, I think that hypothesis is given to over-simplification. In CB28, Alan Townsin added his (considerable) force to the discussion. Ultimately, his take on the subject sided with that of Geoff Burrows; four-bay construction was an AEC-led, or driven, style. But was it?

I don't think anyone disputes that the first 'modern' four-bay double-decker body was that built by Charles H Roe on an AEC Regent chassis and exhibited at the 1937 Commercial Motor Show as

During the postwar years, Maidstone & District had all of its austerity fleet of Bristol, Daimler and Guy buses rebodied. With one exception the new bodies were supplied by Weymann; most were of five-bay construction but in 1953 was supplied a number with this handsome four-bay version. M&D Bristol K6A no.DH140 loads in the bus station at Lower Stone Street, Maidstone, in March 1958.
All photos by Michael Dryhurst except where credited otherwise

Leeds City Transport no.400; did this design have an effect on the stylists at Chiswick? Surely, it must have done. But Roe did not then proceed to build numerous four-bay bodies – far from it. In fact, apart from LPTB RT1-151, Leeds City Transport/Roe no.500 and a handful of Duple-bodied Leyland Titan for Barton Transport, no other examples of four-bay construction were to be seen until after World War 2. And then not in a consistent manner, but yes, with AEC in the majority.

39 companies

By the time post-WW2 bus construction resumed on a large scale, there were some 39 companies in Britain offering double-deck bodywork; in some cases the offerings were new designs, while some companies were merely updating their prewar styles. And some had in their catalogue the four-bay look, and others didn't. And on looking back at over 50 years of the 'four/five' conundrum, there does not appear to be any rhyme nor reason in the application of the styles, although quite often the riddle does come back to AEC. Kent and Sussex were BET strongholds, with East Kent and Maidstone & District in the former, and, of course, Southdown in the latter. In the postwar period all three companies embarked on huge rebodying programmes, with the EKRCC and SMS applying this to prewar double-deckers, while M&D undertook to rebodying its utility fleet (and all three companies took Beadle 'recycled' Regents and Titans as coaches) . While between them, the EKRCC and SMS employed some six bodybuilding companies on this work, with a single exception M&D

Top: *Glasgow Corporation Transport operated 20 Sunbeam F4A trolleybuses, all of which carried four-bay bodies, those on TG1-5 by Alexander, TG6-20 being bodied by Weymann. TG15 of the latter batch is seen here, in February 1960.*

Above: *Bond introduced a double-decker design in the mid-1950s, which was another to favour five-bay design; principal customers were a couple of Lancashire municipals, amongst them Bolton, Bond-bodied Titan PD2 no.71 being seen here (the '8' on the cab door refers to the width).*

used only one: Weymann. Now, excluding its part in the RT programme, Weymann had been building four-bay bodies since late 1946 but when the M&D Bristol/Daimler/Guy rebodyings commenced, in 1951, the Weymann products were of five-bay construction; however, by 1953, rebuilt M&D Bristol K6A were receiving a very handsome Weymann body, which while its Weymann heredity was evident, there was considerable RT-influence here, and needless to say, it was of four-bay construction (and fortunately, an example is in preservation). The next new double-deckers received by M&D were Leyland Titan PD2/12 with Weymann bodywork - but of Orion style, and five-bay (despite the fact that at about this time four-bay Orion bodies were in build for Liverpool); two years later came the last M&D halfcab buses, 22 AEC Regent V with Park Royal bodies of . . .four-bay construction. Well, sez the aficionado, they were AEC and when Park Royal built on the Regent III or V, the bodies were only of four-bay construction. Right . . . ?

About 1948, Park Royal introduced a double-decker body of five-bay construction, which always I associate most readily with the Guy Arab III, Guy also producing this same body to PRV design. However, in addition to the Arab III, this five-bay PRV body could be seen on Arab II, Daimler CVG, Leyland PD2 and . . . AEC Regent III; in the latter case, this was on the initial double-decker fleet of Ipswich Corporation, while Edinburgh had the same five-bay body on AEC Regent III, albeit built under licence by Brockhouse as was the same-styled body

Left: While Burlingham built very stylish-looking double-deckers, it did not use four-bay construction, not even on the AEC Regent III, as seen here on Scottish Omnibuses BB94, in St Andrew Square, Edinburgh, in August 1956.

Below: The standard Cravens postwar product was of five-bay construction, in both highbridge and lowbridge format. Sheffield 'A' fleet no.248 is another example of a five-bay Regent III and shows what little reworking Cravens undertook for its version of the London RT.

St Helens Corporation received a couple of batches of Leyland Titan PD2 with four-bay bodywork by D J Davies, on Park Royal frames. While having an obvious PRV/RT lineage, no.112 still manages to display Davies individuality.
John Fozard

for Aberdeen on Daimler CVG. However, this five-bay PRV body did appear in four-bay format, needless to say on the AEC Regent III chassis, with Morecambe and West Bridgford taking examples. Now tell me this, and tell me no more: there was a period of concurrent production of the AEC Regent II, and of the Regent III. Park Royal, and Weymann, each provided bodywork on both two models; why was it, then, that both companies supplied only five-bay bodywork on the Regent II, whereas four-bay on the Regent III? After all, both were AEC. Alan Townsin, your hand was up first!

Obsessed

Having studied – nay, having been obsessed with – this subject for many years, about the only consistency I can detect is the inconsistency of it all! And I came across it by – ignorance! The bus bug hit this old f—t while still pram-ridden (and isn't life strange, I'm at an age where soon I'll be in a pram again . . .) so by the age of 11, I was well into the hobby/obsession, able to detect blind-folded a 'provincial' Regent III from an RT, a K5G from a K6A from a K6B, a PD1 from a PD2 and so on, and I was able to identify readily most makes of bodywork. But when in my eleventh year was delivered to Brighton, Hove & District Bristol K5G no.6407, this bus was a challenge, believe me. It was put to work on route 6, which just so happened to pass St Christopher's Preparatory School, at which I was an (unwilling) pupil, and thus I had plenty of time to study it, which I did as often as possible and usually at the

expense of my scholastic endeavours, which is probably why I had to take Common Entrance twice. Anyway, on studying the beast, I knew no. 6407 was different, very different, but out of sheer dumbness or myopia, or both, I could never work out for myself what the difference was. And, to add insult to injury, it was that 'swot' from Remove who told me; yes, Bruce Foxall, him with only a passing interest in buses, he pointed-out that no.6407 had but four main windows each side (and 51 years later I still don't know which hurt the most, the fact I could not detect it or the fact it was him who told me). But even this revelation plus the fact that Brighton Corporation operated eight Regent III with Weymann four-bay bodies did not focus me on three main pillars. Long-suffering readers of mine might remember Uncle Tim, one-time manager of the Golders Green Hippodrome whose office overlooked the bus station below. One evening in the spring of 1950, there is an RT on the route 58 stand (Golders Green to Archway in those days). Okay, so it is red with cream relief to the upper-deck windows and cantrail band, and it has a roof route-number box, as did every self-respecting RT, but it is different – somehow it is different. As my uncle and I walk across to board a number 28 bus to his home in Kilburn, I stop and look at this RT on the 58.

'You okay?', asked Uncle Tim.

I pointed to the offending RT. 'That thing. There's something different about it and I can't work it out what it is'.

The bus-dabbling Uncle Tim glanced at that RT. 'It's a Craven.' I nodded. I knew there were Craven RTs. My Ian Allan *ABC of London Transport* told me so. There's even a picture of one on page 36, tearing down Buckingham Palace Road while working a duty on the 11 road. 'Right', said I. 'A Craven.'

'Well, my son,' said the bus-dabbling Uncle Tim. 'A Craven is five-bay. There's your difference'.

I knew that! Of course I knew that! I – knew – that! I fumed, I seethed. At my own inadequacy, at my own inability to determine the difference between four and five, this aggro compounded by other less-qualified mortals pointing it out to me, the swot Foxall and my own theatre-managing uncle. And, this at a time when I could tell a new Park Royal-bodied RT from a Weymann one (it was to do with the shaping of the beading under the cab window). Maybe that's why I've had this ongoing fascination with four- and five-bay double-deckers, it's all to do with the deep inner-self, the sense of failure and the associated self-recrimination and attendant self-loathing combined with the overpowering need to redeem oneself to one's peers. Redeem! Was Freud for five-bay or four? Will we, will I, ever know? Vienna only ever bought long, three-axled double-deckers, so yet again one of life's prevailing mysteries . . . no answer from Sigmund there, and there's little point in having a seance in order to talk to Goethe, because Berlin 'deckers were long also. Rackham!

This July 1963 view of Bristol Omnibus no.C3436 makes a doubly-interesting comparison. One, the full-length four bays, and two, how 'fussy' is the look of the standard five-bay ECW body on the bus in front.

There's the key: Rackham! The Leyland traitor who realised that 'AEC ' was an acronym for 'An Excellent Company' and jumped ship – bus – accordingly, he is the progenitor of my torment with his exhortation concerning double-deck bodies for the AEC Q-type - 'You can have as many windows per side as you like, as long as there are only three main pillars'. Seances can be very long-drawn-out affairs; maybe I could contact Rackham on the Internet, you know, 'AEC four-bay.com'. Or, failing that, one could take a look at the postwar double-decker providers and try to categorise them into 'Four Bay/Five Bay?'; I will try, but I don't think it will point the way, except possibly back to AEC . . .

Alphabetically

Right, we – I – will do this alphabetically. Alexander. Here, the initial postwar offerings showed a marked resemblance to the Leyland product (surprise, surprise) and thus were of five-bay construction, but in the early 1950s Alexander introduced a new double-decker design, which came in both four- and five-bay format. W Alexander & Sons had some Titan PD2 Leylands with this design, in lowbridge configuration and to four-bay build, and very handsome they were, too, yet the rebodied CWA6 of West Bromwich were to five-bay layout. Edinburgh took this design on rebodied CW-series chassis and also on Guy Arab IV, and these latter were very good-looking buses, in four-bay format. Glasgow took this Alexander body on both Daimler CVG and Leyland PD2 chassis (no Southall association here?) but, mucho, mucho more significantly, Glasgow took this four-bay body on TG1-5, Sunbeam F4A trolleybuses; the significance being that these were not only the first trolleybus bodies to be built by Alexander, but also they were the first four-bay trolleybuses in the UK, thus putting paid to that old wives' tale put forward on page 31 of CB25. TG6-20 were a further fifteen F4A trolleybuses, this time with Weymann bodywork – but of four-bay construction!

But Glasgow, Glasgow is a prime example in the inconsistency of preference for 'four bay vs five-bay'. In the 14-year period 1946-60, this fascinating fleet took delivery of double-deck chassis from AEC , Albion, Crossley, Daimler and Leyland, and in addition to bodies for the foregoing, rebodied a number of prewar, and wartime, chassis. GCT received five-bay bodies from Alexander (on chassis as diverse as Leyland Titan TD4 and AEC Regent V!), Crossley, MCCW, Northern Coachbuilders, Roberts and Weymann! (on AEC Regent III, but to MCCW design) and four-bay bodies from Alexander, Brockhouse, Croft, East Lancs, Mann Egerton, Roberts, Scottish Aviation and Weymann. See what I mean, about the 'consistency of the inconsistency'?

Now, where we were we? According to my records, Ashcroft built but five double-decker bodies; and, you might well ask – Ashcroft? A Merseyside firm that supplied some bodies to Birkenhead, and as there were only five, naturally, they were to five-bay. Barnard produced a well-proportioned body with undertones of NCB styling; one's recollection is that most of these were built on Daimler CV-series chassis, and none was four-bay. Beadle; four-bay? Forget it! This company was still building six-bay up until 1950! Despite entering the full-time market in the mid-1950s, whether shaken or stirred, Bond could only offer five-bay format whereas Brockhouse would offer whichever configuration was fancied, seemingly without being inhibited by chassis make, PRV-licensing notwithstanding. Brush swept clean of the four-bay format (except when it came to big-time customer BMMO) as did Burlingham, Cravens and Crossley. Crossley! I hear you say? Yes, Crossley. Crossley produced bodies in two styles, those that were 'home-grown' and those which were operator-inspired; within the latter category fall the Crossley bodies built for Liverpool, all to four-bay construction, hardly surprising as apart from a batch of all-Leyland-built PD2, every LCPT bus from about 1948 to 1958 (Ken Swallow, give me latitude here!) was of four-bay construction, and didn't they benefit from it? The Stockport company supplied 'Liverpool/Crossley' four-bay bodies also to Rotherham and Sheffield, whereas the home-grown

The only Crossley chassis to be bodied by East Lancs were eight for Eastbourne Corporation; numbered 32-9, these DD42/5 buses had four-bay bodywork.

In 1949 London Transport took delivery of a Guy Arab III with a view to possibly building an RT-styled version; in the event, delivery improved of RT-family buses from AEC and Leyland so the Guy option was not pursued, but East Kent FFN 367 gives a clear indication of what would have been the look of an 'RTG'? This is an Arab III the Park Royal body of which owes a great deal to the RT.

Crossley standard was of five-bay construction; Southport had some such Crossley bodies mounted on AEC Regent III - but still they were to five-bay format.

Contrariness

Being completely Welsh on the Da's side, I know about the lively contrariness of those original Brits. Like D J Davies. Not content with running buses and coaches, this company also built them, especially for the Welsh municipalities, the standard product being of five-bay construction, but as Davies built under licence from Park Royal, you could have such a body built to four-bay format. Apart from operators in the Principality, Burton took Davies/five-bay, St Helens Davies/four-bay. Duple never wavered; from the postwar outset until the cessation of double-decker building in the late 1950s, four bay all the way!

Eastern Coach Works. The standard product was of a well-proportioned pleasing-to-the-eye five-bay double-decker, but in 1949/50, a number of the standard highbridge K-type received bodies of four-bay construction; examples went to BH&D, Bristol, Eastern Counties and York-West Yorkshire. The ensuing KS-style was built to four-bay format, but some strange rebodyings saw some KS-characteristics with five-bay format. However, Lowestoft saw the light and the famed Bristol Lodekka LD/LDS/FS/FSF was to four-bay format. ECW is followed by an inconsistency, aka East Lancashire Coachbuilders. As early as 1946, ELCB embraced the four-bay format; the company, and its subsequent subsidiaries, built four-bay bodies on AEC, Bristol, Crossley, Daimler

and Leyland chassis. And then it took fright; around 1950, ELCB and the subsidiaries reverted to the five-bay format, not to be emboldened again until 1967, when it supplied to Bury Corporation some forward-entrance Leyland PD2 with fine-looking bodywork of four-bay format. Another 'Averse-to-Four-Bay' was Harkness of Belfast, which brings us to Leyland. No four-bay there, sez you. Right. If one excludes the 500 RTW bodies built for London Transport. An interesting aside here is the fact that the RT-look influenced not only the subsequent designs of RT builders such as Park Royal, Saunders and Weymann but also a number of other bodybuilders – while not affecting the look of Leyland designs. Maybe the cessation of bodybuilding by Leyland was already on the corporate cards during the time that the RTW bodies were being built?

Longwell Green. I don't recall any four-bay designs out of this company, but did I read recently that this company built on Park Royal frames; if so, were they of four-bay? Lydney Coachworks was the in-house coachbuilding subsidiary of the Red & White group, which occasionally supplied product outside that group, a batch of Leyland PD2 for Leigh springing to mind. These lowbridge buses were of five-bay layout but Lydney did build some four-bay buses, albeit on Weymann frames and on AEC Regent III chassis. Massey Bros, ah, another inconsistency. Like Great Yarmouth Corporation. This operator took identical Massey bodywork on both AEC and Leyland chassis. There was a mix of four- and five-bay styles; no prizes for guessing which was mounted on what? And highlighting once again that AEC/four-bay link?

In 1953, Colchester Corporation took delivery of nos.10-12, AEC Regent III with very elegant four-bay Massey bodies; all subsequent Colchester deliveries were of the AEC/Massey/four-bay combination; until was received some Leyland PD2. With bodywork by Massey – to five-bay format.

Operator-inspired

The Metropolitan Cammell Carriage & Wagon Co, known better by the acronym MCCW, was not a four-bay advocate; unless operator-inspired. 450 RT-style bodies for LTE plus one for Coventry, and 350 D7 four-bay bodies for BMMO; to which must be added the Leyland Lowloader PDRI/LFDD plus those Orion-style bodies to four-bay format after Weymann had ceased business. Unless any of the milk-floats produced by NCB were to four-bay format, I don't think Northern Coachbuilders built any bus bodies of four-bay construction. But Northern Counties did, lots of them. But only for those operators which specified them. For example, similar NCME bodywork was supplied both to Lancashire United, and Southdown; four-bay to Atherton, five-bay to Steine Street. Although, it is relevant to point out that the one-and-only four-bay body ever supplied to SMS was built by NCME. But in retrospect Northern Counties was another of those 'jobbing' coachbuilders - 'you name it, we'll build it'. Which

Yes, yet another AEC Regent III with five-bay bodywork – in this instance Aberdare UDC no.81, one of a batch of four such NCME-bodied buses, three of which went to Aberdare and the other to Bedwas & Machen UDC.

brings us to Park Royal. Which besides the various examples cited previously, built also on AEC Regent chassis a mix of four- and five-bay bodies, instances which spring to mind being supplied to Great Northern Railway (Ireland) and Nottingham City Transport. And PRV supplied to Southdown some 60 bodies of RT-style; but these were on Guy Arab lV and Leyland PD2/12 chassis, so naturally were of five-bay layout. Pickering, four-bay? No way. Reading? If you asked; the standard for this Portsmouth-based company was a five-bay construction body, but Jersey Motor Transport had some four-bay Reading bodies on Leyland Titan 'tin-front' chassis, and West Bridgford on AEC Regent V. And as I never saw them I can't comment, but I seem to recall that Wake's Services of Sparkford, Somerset, had some AEC Regent III bodied by Reading; four- or five-bay? In the initial postwar period, Roberts produced a rather old-fashioned, five-bay body; this was superseded by a four-bay design that was built not only on the AEC Regent III but was supplied also on Daimler, Guy and Leyland, in both highbridge and lowbridge layout.

Dundee Corporation was a four-bay/five-bay mix. Of the former is this Daimler CVG6, with Park Royal bodywork, of a style which was also built by Crossley.

Charles H Roe Ltd, Crossgates Works, Leeds – another enigma. The prewar innovations of which have been noted previously; but how on earth could this company progress (regress?) from that earth-shattering design of 1937 to what was on offer from 1946 to 1951? If I had read the 'Roe' history written by my old buddy Geoff Lumb, I might find the answer; if I could afford it I might know the answer. Roe, of course, built the famous teak-framed body with that trademark waistrail; its forays into metal-framed bodies were usually on Park Royal frames and thus tended to be of four-bay construction, but looked about as much 'Roe' as Roger Moore looked 'Bond'. But it was only a matter of time before Crossgates got it right, as witness the 'Pullman' bodies for Leeds City Transport – ah, magnificent! Oh, they were on AEC Regent III chassis? So they were. But Roe products from about 1952 onwards were, in the (failing) eyes of this yet-to-grow-up geriatric, smashing. And mostly of four-bay construction, while not being limited to AEC chassis. From memory, not Geoff's book, apart from AEC, the Roe four-bay body could be found on Daimler CVG, Guy Arab IV and Leyland PD2 chassis; there was a concurrent trolleybus version, supplied to Ashton, Derby, Doncaster, Maidstone, Teesside and Wolverhampton. Five-bay, natch.

Saunders. This company knew a good thing when it saw one. Producing initially a sort of 'prewar' five-bay leftover design which found its way on to 40 Bristol K6A for Maidstone & District and some 10 rebodied Leyland various TD-Titan for Southdown, the Welsh company was approached by LTE to build for the RT programme; the original plan was to replicate that original five-bay M&D/SMS design as an RT. Fortunately, Welsh good-taste prevailed and not only did we get a Celtic RT, but subsequent Saunders double-deckers showed the RT heritage, including the only rear-engined double-decker to have been bodied at Beaumaris. In preservation is OKM 317, in the opinion of your scribe, one of the best-looking AEC Regent III that carried a body of RT-derivation; four-bay, did I hear you say? It is.

Nicely proportioned

Strachans (Successors) Ltd. was a 'flip-flop'. The initial postwar double-decker was of five-bay construction (ref the super article in CB32, 'Western SMT and the Strachans mystery') but around 1950

From about 1949 onwards, Strachans built a pleasant-looking four-bay body in both highbridge and lowbridge configuration on a number of different chassis, including Dennis Lance III. Seen here in Colchester in the summer of 1963 is an AEC Regent III of Osborne's of Tollesbury.

this gave way to a nicely-proportioned, obviously RT-derived, four-bay bus; this found favour with many independents, particularly in East Anglia, but was replaced in 1954 by – a five-bay design. And Strachans wonders why it went out of business? In my recollection, and that's not saying much, I don't recall Scottish Aviation as a builder of double-decker bodies, but it was, and mainly for Glasgow Corporation Transport, and to four-bay format. Celtic aestheticism, yet again. And there was another double-deck builder beyond Hadrian's Wall, Scottish Commercial; this company's product appeared to have been inspired by the Crossley 'Manchester' look, and thus was of five-bay format. In retrospect, the next Celtic contender probably would prompt me to disown my Cambrian heredity. Welsh Metal Industries. Mother always maintained the worst thing you could say about anybody was that 'they meant well'. WMI meant well; even down to the five-bay bodies where the glass panes were set in putty. Wilks & Meade tried, but failed; six-bay bodies married to a full-front? In 1950? And then there was Willowbrook. The initial postwar designs, though distinctive and readily recognisable, in a way were sort of, well, bland. But in the mid-1950s, was produced a very impressive and distinctive four-bay body, as can be seen in CB5 page 27. This example is mounted on a Titan PD2/12 chassis; I think East Yorkshire had the same design on AEC Regent

(exposed radiator) MkV. Were there others? Delaine's preserved PD2/20, no.45?

Which brings us to Weymann, in my book, the four-bay champion, operators notwithstanding. Like Aberdeen. 'Provincial' RT in 1947, Weymann four-bay; Daimler CVG6 in 1950, Weymann five-bay. But Bury got it right. Leyland Titan, Weymann five-bay; AEC Regent III, Weymann four-bay. Leyland Titan, Weymann four-bay. Wey(!) to go . . .

On this subject, probably Weymann deserves an article to itself. Suffice to say here that in the humble opinion of your scribe, the aesthetics of a Weymann four-bay body mounted on an AEC Regent III took a lot of beating. Although, in retrospect, those AEC Regent V of Rochdale with what proved to be the ultimate in Weymann four-bay design also were exceptionally well-proportioned and good-looking buses...

But, you know, at the end of the day... four-bay or five-bay? I think it really boiled-down to operator choice, AEC notwithstanding. Look at the two largest Lancashire municipal operators; Liverpool, essentially a four-bay fleet, Manchester – five-bay. **CB**

TODMORDEN'S INDIAN SUMMER

DAVID BEILBY recalls the JOC's last days

APRIL 1971 saw the operations of Todmorden Joint Omnibus Committee taken over by Calderdale Joint Omnibus Committee, a rare case of one municipal operator being taken over by another. However, for a period of around five months there was very little change in Todmorden, apart from fleet renumbering and standard Halifax blinds, and the whole operation retained its distinctive character.

I had always associated Todmorden's fleet with Leyland-bodied PD2s but was not blind to the steady arrival of replacement vehicles in the form of Leyland Leopards. Therefore when the news broke of the takeover it seemed that a visit to photograph the remaining examples had developed an increased urgency. Several visits ensued over the course of that summer which allowed me to become very familiar with the fleet and its operations, although I was pleased that the

prediction of an early demise for the PD2s proved to be far from accurate.

The shape of the town of Todmorden and its bus routes are very much dictated by the topography of the area, in that steep-sided valleys from the south and the north-west converge and head eastwards as the Calder. In these valleys are the principal road and rail links from the town to Rochdale, Burnley and Halifax respectively. The core services have always been based on these three corridors, which to this day still see both road and rail links.

In 1971 the services ran at 20-minute intervals on the

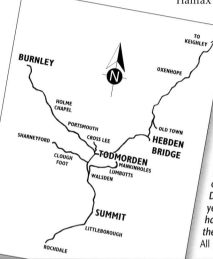

Although all-Leyland PD2/12 no.352 is showing Summit on the blind as it passes Steanor Bottom it is actually on a journey extended towards Littleborough to the Sladen Wood mill of Fothergill & Harvey, a firm that David Beilby was to work for some 13 years later. However, on this occasion he had to follow the bus to find out where the working went!
All photos by David Beilby

Above: *Hebden Bridge's station building makes an attractive backdrop as no.355 (KWX 17) waits to depart for Keighley on 10 July 1971.*

Left: *The oldest member of the fleet was all-Leyland PD2/1 no.351 (HWY 36), new in January 1950 as no.18, a corporation-owned vehicle. It is seen climbing through Portsmouth on the way to Burnley.*

three main routes, connecting in the town centre bus station which was below the viaduct carrying the railway. In the direction of Rochdale the service terminated at Littleborough Summit, where you connected with Rochdale Corporation route 6A (or sometimes the 6) to get to that town. I say connected, but with the best will in the world it is difficult to engineer good connections between one service running every 15 minutes and the other

every 20. It was possible to travel on a through bus, but by 1971 this was only on a Saturday afternoon. This link was given the number 20 by Rochdale (Todmorden didn't use service numbers) but in latter years was worked exclusively by Todmorden.

Connections

Through buses to Burnley only ran every 40 minutes, alternate journeys terminating at a place called Portsmouth not easily confused, except in name, with its much larger south coast namesake. The Hebden Bridge service was straightforward and allowed connection at the outer end with Halifax JOC services 48 and 49 to Halifax and Brighouse. It was only possible to catch a through bus to Halifax if you were at school or visiting hospital. These Halifax routes were regularly worked by the superb Dennis Loline IIIs that featured Gardner 6LX engines, five-speed semi-automatic transmission, air suspension at the rear and coach seating. This batch, the last Lolines built, went to West Riding when still young to help eliminate the troublesome Wulfrunians.

There were other services, which will be referred to in due course, but the three mentioned above were the principal sources of traffic for the fleet. They

Leyland PD2/12 no.354 returns to Todmorden from Summit on 10 July 1971.

were not operated as separate routes but worked through the town centre, although through fares were not available. Interworking of vehicles was not confined to these three routes and if you chose carefully you could get on a bus and remain on it for a tour of most of the network, as I did at times. It also therefore follows that it was possible to see most types of bus on each route, adding to the interest.

Todmorden Corporation had the distinction of being the second local authority in the country (after Eastbourne) to operate its own bus services, having decided against its original intention of operating electric tramways. Two Critchley-Norris open-top double-deckers started operation in December 1906 and the trunk routes along each valley bottom were quickly established. Todmorden soon learnt that Leyland made better buses than Critchley-Norris and Ryknield and never bought another make new after 1907. Fleet growth was gradual, however, until the 1920s, when new services were started and existing services expanded.

The Joint Omnibus Committee came into being in 1931 and resulted in half the fleet being owned by the Corporation and the other half by the Joint Omnibus Committee. The railways obviously took little interest in later years as the garter of the LMS Railway (nationalised on 1 January 1948) could still

to be seen on some JOC vehicles in the late 1960s, although it had been replaced by the simple text 'British Railways' or the BR double-arrow logo on the all the operational fleet by the takeover. The operation was technically joint between the Corporation and Amalgamated Passenger Transport Limited at the time of takeover.

By 1971 the fleet was mainly single-deck, with 15 Leyland Leopards carrying bodies by East Lancs, Willowbrook and Pennine. These were accompanied by two Tiger Cubs with Weymann bodywork, an unusual secondhand purchase from East Midland. Three of the unique ECW-bodied Leopards had been acquired in late 1970, these having originated in the Sheffield 'C' fleet which was owned by British Railways. They very quickly moved to Halifax after the takeover and do not feature in this story. The double-deck fleet, however, was the main centre of interest as it comprised seven Leyland-bodied PD2s, all of which were about 20 years old. What made the interest greater is that this was no reserve fleet for school specials and peak-hour journeys, but used in all-day service and liable to appear on any route.

All all-Leyland

The fleet did, for a short time I believe, achieve the distinction in being 100% composed of Leyland-bodied PD2s. The 40 of the type purchased were the mainstay of the fleet for a very long time. Eight were PD2/12s with Leyland's last standard-style bodies, the remainder being the shorter and narrower PD2/1 model. The bodies on all these vehicles were of the lowbridge type. A bridge on the Burnley road once necessitated the use of such vehicles but following its rebuilding in the 1930s highbridge vehicles could pass freely over Todmorden's routes. Unfortunately the fiscally-prudent transport department had not seen any advantage in putting a few more courses of bricks in the depot walls before they put the roof on. Even today, despite some rebuilding, the depot does not allow free access for full-height buses and it still influences the design of those based at Todmorden.

To see what Todmorden was about, let us take a journey I made on 11 September 1971. We arrive at Littleborough Summit on what was Rochdale's first Fleetline, now in orange as Selnec no.6223. The bus onwards is one of the Pennine-bodied Leopards carrying the Calderdale fleetnumber 332. I am not too concerned that it is not a PD2 as it is my fourth visit to the town in the past week and I am a little more selective in my requirements. (I have had a hectic week as it has also included visits to the Midlands and Perth/Fife!)

Despite the placename the descent from Summit to Todmorden is very gradual, initially through an open valley accompanied only by the canal, for the railway is beneath us in the notorious Summit tunnel. We soon pass the old tollhouse at the rural location of Steanor Bottom. This unlikely spot was the original terminus of the Summit route, simply because it was the boundary. Common sense later

On 4 August 1971 the author was in Todmorden with the preserved Bury Regent III no.77 (BEN 177) publicising the Trans-Pennine Run when he was treated to the remarkable spectacle of no fewer than six of the seven PD2s in the bus station at the same time – the missing example being no.356. No.355 can just be seen displaying its new Calderdale livery.

prevailed and the link to the Rochdale tram terminus was made. The remainder of the journey through Walsden is unremarkable.

Once in Todmorden we wait hopefully at the Hebden Bridge stop and our luck is in, as at around 1.30pm no.356, one of the PD2/12s, rolls into the bus station with Keighley on the blind. This is not an incorrectly set blind, as I thought the first time I saw it, but probably Todmorden's most interesting route.

Our bus started life as fleetnumber 25 and was one of the vehicles owned by the corporation. At the end of the month it will have completed 20 years in service and will see another two before withdrawal. It is a warm and sunny day, no.356 looks very smart, still in the Todmorden livery of dark green and cream, unlike sister no.355 which caused some astonishment the previous month when it was repainted into the distinctive Calderdale scheme of orange, green and cream. No.356 was shortly to receive similar treatment.

Unlucky 13

As we head out of Todmorden we pass the lowbridge depot at Millwood. As well as the active fleet there is an additional PD2/12 stored there, the unlucky former no.13, which is used as a source of spares and also as an informal mess room. A more interesting vehicle, which has only just been withdrawn, is the towing bus, which is a 1934 Leyland Tiger TS6 with the remnants of its Northern Counties body. It had carried out this role since withdrawal as far back as 1942.

The route we are following will be familiar to any readers who have participated in the Trans-Pennine Run, as that rally passes from Littleborough Summit through Todmorden and Hebden Bridge. The stretch of the Calder Valley through Eastwood is lovely, being particularly steep-sided and wooded in places. The architecture is familiar to me as Millstone Grit is the predominant building material, just as it is where I live. As we near Hebden Bridge the valley becomes a gorge and the river, canal and road occupy what is left of the valley floor, leaving the railway to leap across all three on the splendid Whiteley's Viaduct, a stone construction with elegant cast iron spans. This part of the valley was described by Cobbett as ' . . the most interesting that I ever saw . . . it is here where nature has been sportive, indeed.'

Hebden Bridge is starting to become a popular tourist attraction but developed during the Industrial Revolution, making its own niche in the manufacturing of fustian, a type of cotton used in the production of corduroy. Houses cling to the sides of the hill and there are many double-deck houses here, four storey buildings with doors at the front on the ground floor and at the back, facing the hill, on the second floor.

Our bus does not turn into the usual terminal point, instead it carries on through the town and turns right down a narrow road to the station. According to the fare table the fare should be one penny more to this point but the conductor is not too strict on this point. In fact he keeps lowering our age until we are only paying half-fare and as the day progresses he doesn't always even bother with that.

Unspoiled

Hebden Bridge was (and is) a beautifully unspoiled station, retaining all its period wooden signs in keeping with the town's current status as an tourist attraction. We wait here a short while for a connecting train before commencing our climb up to

All-Leyland PD2/12 no.356 has backed up to the bus stop at Cross Lee, ready to return to Todmorden. The Halifax bus stop sign can be clearly seen.

West Yorkshire doing a morning return trip and Todmorden doing the afternoon one.

On arrival at Hebden Bridge station there is a Pennine-bodied Leopard, no.333, waiting to go to Old Town. This bus has already received the Calderdale livery. We will see it return before we depart as we have a long layover here. As the route to Old Town shares much with the one on which we have travelled there is little to describe. The terminus is fairly nondescript, the bus reversing round the corner of a mill.

Having by now got used to 356 we stay with it as it returns to Hebden Bridge and Todmorden and speculate where it will be going next. We know, of course, because the conductor has told us we are due a trip to Cloughfoot. Our luck is definitely in as this route only has six workings on a Saturday. The route runs through a very narrow defile along the road to Bacup.

Inhospitable

Todmorden once ran a through service to that town and even worked a Bacup to Burnley service. Both these services passed over wild and inhospitable moors and were probably never very remunerative. Todmorden had ceased operation of both a few years earlier than our visit but retained a vestigial service along the Bacup road as far as Cloughfoot with two journeys on Mondays to Fridays extended, just broaching the summit at Sharneyford. I had travelled up there only four days earlier on 357, another PD2/12, and experienced the strange sight of Temperley's fireclay works with its huge stockpile of clay pipes and fittings creating a surreal orange landscape. Through passengers to Bacup had to change at Sharneyford to a Ribble or a Rossendale bus at what must be one of the most inhospitable interchanges in the country, on the top of bleak hills at 1,250ft.

Our bus leaves Todmorden on the Rochdale road and turns off towards Bacup under Gauxholme viaduct, another impressive structure on the railway that contains an identical cast iron span to the one seen earlier but this time featuring crenellations. The valley is wooded and sparsely populated and we soon reach the hamlet of Cloughfoot. The bus reverses here into a special area marked by a sign lettered 'Bus Turning Point' in a style similar to that used on Todmorden's bus stops. The latter, sadly, have already disappeared and been replaced by the distinctive Halifax ones coloured green for a bus stop and orange for a fare stage. Todmorden obviously had some difficulty in this remote valley finding names for all

Pecket Well and Crimsworth. The initial part of the climb is amongst houses but we then enter Pecket Wood whose thick foliage prevents us looking down towards Hardcastle Crags. In the wood we pass a bus descending from Old Town. This route diverges at Pecket Well by a very sharp right turn, so much so that a turning area is built out from the road on the left to give buses room to make the manoeuvre.

We keep to the main road and are rewarded by some superb views down the valley and across to Heptonstall on the hillside beyond. The road climbs inexorably and the scenery gets bleaker as we see clearly from where the atmosphere of Wuthering Heights comes. Finally, at an altitude of just over 1,400ft, the climb is over, although our PD2 has taken it all in its stride. The road now descends steeply with a lot of curves so the driver needs to concentrate on this stretch. Once in Oxenhope the descent becomes more steady all the way to Keighley and we are able to watch activities on the Keighley & Worth Valley Railway for most of the rest of the journey.

Our bus looks most incongruous in Keighley bus station, surrounded as it is by the much more modern red and cream buses of West Yorkshire and the joint company set up by West Yorkshire and Keighley Corporation, Keighley-West Yorkshire. These fleets are in the process of being renumbered and the distinctive vehicle identities that involved up to four letters as well as numbers are being replaced by ordinary four-digit numbers. It would seem that computers can't cope with identities like KSMA4.

We return with the bus to Hebden Bridge, the conductor having checked first that we are on board (the crews were like that). It is important that we don't miss it though, as there are only two through journeys each way a day and we are on the second! The route is actually the only normal one of Todmorden's that is jointly operated, with Keighley-

ENGINE OIL

TODMORDEN JOINT OMNIBUS COMMITTEE

TODMORDEN CORPORATION

The Todmorden Joint Omnibus Committee device, carried by one of the ex-East Midland Tiger Cubs. (The East Midland fleetname can be seen under the paintwork.)

the fare stages as the one above Cloughfoot is simply shown in the fare table as Stage 9 (which it was!).

We return to Todmorden for our final exploration, which is probably the least interesting route to Cross Lee estate. Despite the name the route is worked, of course, by Leylands! It is only a short service and involves a fair degree of twisting and turning down back streets. On our return to town we get off no.356 and bid farewell, having been on the bus for four and a half hours. After all that travelling it is quite nice to get on board no.328 for the return to Summit as it is one of the two Pennine-bodied Leopards with dual-purpose seating.

There is only one route not so far mentioned which is the one serving the delightfully-named hamlets of Lumbutts and Mankinholes, which lie in the hills under Stoodley Pike, a prominent local war memorial. Access to this area was difficult by bus and the only suitable road made an acute angle with the Rochdale road. As a result buses had to continue about a mile further on, to Walsden, to turn round. These routes were the least frequent and the only ones on which I never travelled on a PD2 – I once arrived in Todmorden just as a PD2 was leaving for Mankinholes, so it did happen.

The Burnley route is not to form part of our itinerary on this trip but such an important route cannot be ignored, particularly as it had its own distinctive character. Leaving Todmorden it climbs steadily up the valley, which becomes very narrow, leaving railway, road, houses and mills in intimate proximity. After Portsmouth the scenery becomes much more rural. We cross over the railway at Copy

Pit summit, a mecca for enthusiasts in the last years of British Railways steam as they flocked to see 8Fs slogging up the bank from Burnley with freight for West Yorkshire.

Our bus enters the district of Cliviger and passes through the two villages of Holme Chapel and Walk Mill. A short climb brings us up to a junction with the road from Bacup along which Todmorden's buses used to run. We descend quite sharply past the Towneley terminus and look to see if a Burnley Colne & Nelson bus is waiting there. Restrictions apply on the Todmorden service from this point and our bus is not allowed to pick up any more passengers. Burnley is still of great interest at this time as the fleet contains an interesting variety of vehicles, but these will have to wait until another time.

Todmorden's Indian Summer turned to autumn at the end of September 1971, when a completely new service pattern was introduced. There is no doubt that the changes were beneficial to the public as they removed a lot of the artificial boundaries that existed. However, the character of the organisation was lost and the buses ceased to have that something special about them. Nonetheless, partly due to the constraints imposed by the depot, the services around Todmorden tended to be worked by distinctive vehicles.

The years following the takeover provided much of interest in both the operation and the vehicles and this story will be told in a later issue of *Classic Bus* magazine. **CB**

The interior of the lower deck of all-Leyland PD2/1 no.352, the combination of polished woodwork and leather giving the interior a gorgeous atmosphere on a warm summer afternoon.

TODMORDEN JOINT OMNIBUS COMMITTEE FLEET LIST AT TAKEOVER

Fleet No.		Reg. No.	Chassis	Body	In service	Notes
H/x	Tod					
321	2	1880 WA	Leyland Leopard L1	ECW C41F	31.7.70	Ex-Sheffield
322	3	1881 WA	Leyland Leopard L1	ECW C41F	1.8.70	Ex-Sheffield
323	13	1882 WA	Leyland Leopard L1	ECW C41F	1.8.70	Ex-Sheffield
324	4	NWW 88E	Leyland Leopard PSU4/1R	Willowbrook B45F	1.2.67	
325	9	NWW 89E	Leyland Leopard PSU4/1R	Willowbrook B45F	1.2.67	
326	1	NWW 90E	Leyland Leopard PSU4/1R	Willowbrook DP43F	1.2.67	
327	10	NWW 91E	Leyland Leopard PSU4/1R	Willowbrook DP43F	1.2.67	
328	6	BWU 688H	Leyland Leopard PSU4A/2R	Pennine DP43F	1.12.69	
329	8	BWU 689H	Leyland Leopard PSU4A/2R	Pennine DP43F	1.12.69	
330	14	BWU 690H	Leyland Leopard PSU4A/2R	Pennine B45F	1.12.69	
331	19	BWU 691H	Leyland Leopard PSU4A/2R	Pennine B45F	1.11.69	
332	22	BWU 692H	Leyland Leopard PSU4A/2R	Pennine B45F	1.11.69	
333	23	BWU 693H	Leyland Leopard PSU4A/2R	Pennine B45F	1.11.69	
334	12	634 WY	Leyland Leopard L1	East Lancs B43F	1.4.61	
335	16	520 BWT	Leyland Leopard L1	East Lancs B42F	1.9.62	
336	31	521 BWT	Leyland Leopard L1	East Lancs B44F	1.9.62	
337	29	572 EYG	Leyland Leopard L1	East Lancs B44F	1.1.64	
338	37	573 EYG	Leyland Leopard L1	East Lancs B44F	1.1.64	
339	11	URR 355	Leyland Tiger Cub PSUC1/1	Weymann B44F	26.7.69	Ex-East Midland
340	15	VAL 366	Leyland Tiger Cub PSUC1/1	Weymann B44F	26.7.69	Ex-East Midland
351	18	HWY 36	Leyland Titan PD2/1	Leyland L27/26R	1.1.50	
352	5	JWY 824	Leyland Titan PD2/1	Leyland L27/26R	1.11.50	
353	7	KWX 12	Leyland Titan PD2/12	Leyland L27/26R	1.10.51	
354	20	KWX 14	Leyland Titan PD2/12	Leyland L27/26R	1.10.51	
355	24	KWX 17	Leyland Titan PD2/12	Leyland L27/26R	1.10.51	
356	25	KWX 18	Leyland Titan PD2/12	Leyland L27/26R	1.10.51	
357	27	KWX 19	Leyland Titan PD2/12	Leyland L27/26R	1.10.51	

47 VARIETIES

ROBERT E JOWITT, with a few historical notes for the sake of putting the rest of his essay in context, then sets forth on a nostalgia trip over Hants & Dorset's route 47, as he knew it – and the several curious visitors which sometimes served it and its adjacent routes – from the late 1950s to the end of the 1980s, and naturally not without a touch of romantic interest . . .

HANTS & DORSET'S ROUTE 47 or, as it is now, Solent Blue Line's 47, is just another average bus route, with the same sort of chequered past as any other long-lived route. I would not favour it with a second glance, were it not that it provided a piece of backdrop – as any good bus route should, in anyone's life! – for some or three and above all one of my many relationships with what is known in unsupportive sisterhood terms as the fair sex and at the same time, in this backdrop, produced an amazing vehicular variety.

Let us start with necessary but thoroughly boring history, or as much as we need of it to set the scene, and get it out of the way as fast as possible. Probably every reader knows it anyway. Back in the palmy days before World War 1 a firm of charabancs and motor omnibuses sprang into existence in Bournemouth and district, and this firm was known in fact as Bournemouth & District. In the less palmy but more expansionist days following the War to End All Wars the firm expanded its territory, mopping up pirates and independents as it did so, and in due season and not without reason changed its title to

Hants & Dorset, by which it remained known until relatively recent years. This change was actually in July 1920, five months after its expansions in the city of Southampton had allowed it to launch an attack of three buses per day in the direction of Winchester, increased later in the year to nine.

We will pass over the next 15 years of the route, except for mentioning that, firstly, in its early years, the bold independent and rapidly expanding motor services of King Alfred or Robert Chisnell of Winchester had a notion of expanding towards Southampton but never actually reached further in this direction than the village of Otterbourne, and, secondly, that in 1927 it (the route, not the village of Otterbourne!) first received a route number – 20 – until we come to 1935. In this year H&D, having acquired property immediately opposite Winchester Guildhall and in cheekily close proximity to King Alfred pavement-side stops below the famous statue of King Alfred, opened a new 'Omnibus Station.' This was marked by the Mayor of Winchester cutting a tape with a pair of gold scissors decorated with a likeness of a Hants & Dorset bus, but marred by a cloudburst and the late arrival of the real bus. While wondering what happened to this covetable pair of scissors afterwards we must move on to 1940 when the number 20 was changed to 47; which, 60 years later, it still is.

Basically the geographical route has remained unchanged since the day it started, following the main road from Southampton to Winchester via the villages of Chandler's Ford and Otterbourne, though the landscape in those 80 years has changed beyond all recognition with mushrooming ribbon development between the wars, the Luftwaffe's efforts on Southampton in World War 2, several alterations to the main roads by the addition of

In a bright May 1960 afternoon H&D no.1324 (LRU 53), a 1952 Bristol KSW6G, plods sedately along St Cross Road towards the centre of Winchester. This scene was so typical and so boring that Jowitt with his Ilford Sportsman would not have taken it save for the fact that the hedge on the right contained the dwelling of one of his girlfriends (not one of those mentioned in the text, but yet another!). All photos by Robert E Jowitt

Above: *Compton Down cutting from the south, with 1957 LD6G no.1399 (UEL 720) approaching the summit. The cutting was originally dug for stagecoaches such as the celebrated Red Rover, and the object of this 1960 scene was that it was about to be swept away to accommodate the northern end of the Chandler's Ford bypass. The position from which the shot was taken would soon thus be in mid-air.*

Below: *Compton Down cutting from the north, with the summit just beyond the furthest vehicles and a pretty new H&D Lodekka heading south. The Atkinson with trailer, the 'big' Bedford and the vans are worth a glance too. The dual carriageway was the south end of the Winchester bypass, built between the wars to relieve unemployment, which at this point narrowed to the old main-road cutting. The building of the Chandler's Ford bypass as an extension involved the removal of the war memorial (visible top right of bus) with a good deal of ecclesiastical hassle, and then some three decades later the whole landscape was upheaved and dug out even more again with the conversion to the M3. Mary's house was up behind the pines on the right.*

HANTS AND DORSET MOTOR SERVICES LTD
— OMNIBUS STATION —

Last days of Lodekkas on the 47 in May 1980. H&D KRU 240F pauses – or poses – below the 1935 portal of the 'Omnibus Station' in Winchester. Both the fleetname and the word 'omnibus' were soon to disappear from this vantage point, following Lodekkas into oblivion.

roundabouts and bypasses from the 1950s onwards plus further spreading of housing estates, and most recently the disruption of huge segments of landscape and human lives with motorway construction.

Boring Bristols

I suppose that it was in the mid-to-late 1940s that I first came to know the route, and I vaguely recall a camp full of German prisoners-of-war adjacent to it, between Hut Hill and Chandler's Ford, but I cannot say I took a lot of notice of the buses. In the first place the family had a car, secondly I was much more interested in trains, and thirdly, by the time I came to know anything about buses, those of Hants & Dorset were basically boring Bristols. It was not

From the demise of King Alfred in April 1973 the streets of Winchester were graced with antique H&D buses to replace newer KA buses withdrawn as unfit. These veterans never worked the 47 – though they may well have done so in their prime – and here we see no.1384 (formerly no.1321) a KSW6G all of 20 years old passing the shop where the founder of King Alfred Motor Services, Mr Robert Chisnell, founded the basis of his fortune by selling sausages, potatoes and onions to the troops encamped round Winchester in World War 1. This particular bus was known on account of its advertisement as 'The Tamarind Seed' and on the strength of the advert, years later, Jowitt picked up a copy of the book for 5p on a junk stall; it proved quite a good read!

until the late 1950s that route 47 began to glow in a romantic light. On 10 April 1958, at a charity ball for teenagers – waltzes, quicksteps, the eightsome reel and the Gay Gordons to a three-piece band – I met Mary. She was, I believe, barely a teenager, but the most attractive creature imaginable, with glossy black hair, large brown eyes and adorably turned-up nose. We wrote chaste letters to each other for a year – she was a boarder at a convent school and letters were liable to censorship! – and in the hols she sometimes came over to have tea. She lived at a place called Compton Down, on a hill overhanging the 47, (much of the hill though not her house now bulldozed out of existence by the contentious M3 extension) so her trips into Winchester involved her catching the 47 and then, when we met at the library, carrying on by a King Alfred, usually a Leyland halfcab single-decker. Both King Alfred and Hants & Dorset buses thus suddenly became crowned with haloes of passion. At the end of the year, on 7 April 1959, she was my partner at the repeat of the charity ball. That was the only time I kissed her . . . as a forfeit at the behest of the bandmaster. Then she wrote abruptly saying she wasn't going to write any more; and to this day, though I saw her often enough at subsequent dances, I have never found out her reason. Mary, if by some unlikely chance you read these words, write and tell me why!

My feelings for Mary will be accepted by regular readers as in true Jowitt style. Other readers may care to dismiss them as romantic nonsense and irrelevant, but let it here be noted that one of the buses on which Mary travelled home after one of these tea parties was no.1145, its number graven on my heart.

This vehicle was something of a rarity, being a 1947 Leyland PD1A, one of a batch of seven (1145 – 1151, GLJ 957etc, with ECW lowbridge body.) At this date and apart from these seven there were only six other Leylands (1949 PD2s) and six 1948 AEC Regent IIIs in the nearly-all-Bristol fleet.

Following the rupture from Mary came also a ten year rupture from Winchester when my family removed to New Milton, and a prolonged dose of Hants & Dorset Bristols of various types, before I re-established myself in Winchester where the H&D Bristols on the 47 and other routes out of Winchester proved no more exciting than their counterparts in New Milton in face of the delights provided by the still proudly independent King Alfred.

Intolerable

Alas, however, the charms of King Alfred were already burning away like the famous cakes. This was due to many reasons, not least the dreadful traffic congestion in Winchester. Until the northern extension of the bypass was completed this was intolerable, and afterwards it was very soon almost as intolerable again. Buses coming in along Southgate Street could be delayed by heaven-knows-how-many turns of the traffic lights, buses going out via North Walls ditto ditto. Keeping to the timetable was a joke, but not a very funny one, and a big problem so far as the operation of route 47 was concerned.

I have written much on the demise of King Alfred elsewhere, so will not repeat myself on the matter save only to say that when Hants & Dorset took over the operations of King Alfred in April 1973 it encountered a serious vehicle shortage. It may be

Another 47 variety, undated alas, was provided by a visitor from across the water, this one more in keeping with the normal run of 47 vehicles at the time, if nevertheless inspiring visions of golden sands at Sandown or the Needles you cannot thread. As it boasts a Southampton depot code spot just left of the grille it may be that it had been bought rather than borrowed, but the Isle of Wight title in front of Barclays Bank in Winchester provides a curious charm for those familiar with Hampshire and the IoW.

deemed partisan to suggest that the quantity of defects H&D engineers found on KA buses amounted to bitchiness; it is absolutely true to say that H&D engineers while in the process of vehicle examination smashed in the side of a perfectly good KA Leyland Panther (I was there as witness to this crime on the spot!) and it is equally true that H&D was already suffering a bus shortage quite apart from KA problems.

To address this shortage a couple of very ancient Bristols were drafted in to serve on Winchester local routes (though not on the 47,) substituting for more recent but defective KA buses, and I can here retail a story I told in *Buses Annual* many years ago. Having just borrowed the KA garage for repainting one of my 1930s Parisian Renault buses – incidentally the last paint-job ever done on KA premises – I took this bus out for a driver-training run round local routes, shortly ahead of a regular schedule, and several optimistic passengers seriously tried to stop it in the belief it was H&D's latest offering . . .

Unlikely vehicles

This really brings me to the subject that I am trying to describe, namely the diversity of unlikely vehicles that turned up on the 47 over the next few years.

For the sake of accuracy I must here mention that H&D had other or alternative routes between Southampton and Winchester, which I have failed to describe in the historical synopsis at the beginning of this essay, and that some of these visitors may have worked on these as well as or rather than on the 47. The main point is that they were all 'a tale of two cities', and to this I could add that whether the general picture of the 47 from 1970 was first of all almost entirely Lodekka or FLF, and then almost

entirely VR, there were moments when it was also Leyland National, for example when Southgate Street in Winchester was closed for two or three months for drainage works and extraordinary diversions required buses to pass under a long-defunct railway low bridge, or in the evenings when a Leyland National was quite adequate for the number of passengers. I shall forever cherish the memory of the hindmost seat on a Leyland National when I and my beloved Margaret (a quarter of a century after I first met Mary) were its only two passengers on a late-evening high speed run on the 47 from Southampton to Winchester. One way and another it was one of the most exciting bus rides I have ever experienced. As for the diversions, I recall a splendid moment when, travelling on a Leyland National 47 round a right angle bend which had pro-tem been declared one-way traffic, we encountered a car – one of many – which had chosen to ignore the pro-tem system; the bus driver very slowly and very carefully and very politely thrust the driver of the oncoming car backwards and deeper and ever more inextricably into the offside bank of the bend until, with the car about to overturn, there was room for the bus to pass . . .

But from these delightful diversions, which were in the 1980s, let us return to the day-to-day operations of the early 1970s. In theory these were, as I have said above, almost entirely Lodekka. In practice this was where the aliens entered. By some curious and un-Jowitt lapse my negatives and diaries for the immediate post-King Alfred period are not maintained in my usual more-or-less orderly fashion; furthermore some of the negatives aren't even very good. I can account for this only by the presence on the scene of a girlfriend, though not any of those

Further variety on the 47, this time quite clear in Jowitt notes and fairly clear in Jowitt photographs, came from Portsmouth, all in the form of 1963/4 Atlantean PDR1/1 vehicles, in 1979. We see in this Winchester view no.224 in Southgate Street on 13 January.

mentioned in these words for this particular one had little or nothing to do with route 47. Not that this stopped me studying it. Anyway, assuming my negatives to be in order if nothing else, the first 'interloper' was a 1959 Metro-Cammell highbridge Leyland PD3/6, STP 997, hired from Portsmouth Corporation Transport. I guess this was in the winter of 1974/5. Next in line, probably, after this unlikely vision of exposed radiator and cream-and-maroon livery, was a good deal more normal, being a Lodekka; the only unusual thing about it was that it said 'Southern Vectis' on its side. Perhaps this was in wintertime too, otherwise it would have been busy rushing around between Newport and Cowes and Ryde and so forth, wouldn't it. Then came a brief spell with an ex-City of Oxford 1958 Park Royal highbridge AEC Regent V, 975 CWL, painted in the livery of Provincial of Fareham, though actually in the ownership of H&D, in the spring of 1975, and this was followed by more Regents Vs borrowed from Devon General.

Rejuvenated

By this time the King Alfred vehicles, rejuvenated and dabbed with yellow and orange depot spots to indicate the code for Winchester, had been assimilated into the H&D fleet; and, one by one, most of them emerged in National Bus poppy red, very horribly. It thus came about, if probably infrequently, that King Alfred buses worked through to Southampton, as their founder had wished they would, if in circumstances far from those he could have foreseen.

So far as my records go, the next serious bus shortage must have occurred in 1979, for here, very accurately, I have Portsmouth Corporation Atlantean no.224 working the 47 on 13 January, no.236 on

30 January, and no.215 on 3 February. These were all from the 1963/4 deliveries, and typical Portsmouth, though certainly less antique than the previous borrowing! I had no notion then – and I still have not now – what sort of understanding there must have been between H&D and PCT, and in truth I don't much care. Sufficient unto the day was such an unusual sight, no call to ask the reason why . . .

The end of the decade more or less coincided with the retreat of the Lodekkas. For ten years I had been walking daily – or almost, hangovers permitting – along Southgate Street, and I was much more interested in Prudence, who also – because she then worked in an office there - frequently walked along Southgate Street, usually in a delicious pair of scarlet high heels, her brown hair trailing down her back and her delightfully tip-tilted nose turned up against the FLF exhaust. I did not then know her name, I found it out later on seeing her photo in the Hampshire Chronicle, and meanwhile I suddenly discovered that the boring Lodekkas were dying and desirable. That's life – or death – isn't it!

Hampshire Bus

In the early 1980s – at the time when Hants & Dorset, for reasons of which every reader of Classic Bus Yearbook should be well aware, came to be known instead as Hampshire Bus - I was working in a shop in Jewry Street. To anyone who is unfamiliar with Winchester I must explain that 47s come into the city via Southgate Street and continue further into it via Jewry Street on their way to the bus station, and that regardless of all the permutations of traffic control which have been applied to the city's streets in the past 30 years this arrangement still persists as it did from the 1920s. In these circumstances I had a regular vision of the revolting

Above: *Poppy-red H&D VR on the 47 in a cloudburst along Jewry Street, Winchester. The white spots on the nearside of the bus are (probably) out-of-focus raindrops falling from the canopy of the greengrocery shop from which Jowitt looked out for the passing of Prudence.*

Right: *In this September 1989 view outside Barclays Bank, Jewry Street, Winchester, we see the Hampshire Bus VR in its final fling on the 47, all immaculate in Stagecoach livery, even if vague about its destination.*

VRs which had cleared the Lodekkas off the 47, and also a regular vision of Prudence who had now abandoned her job in Southgate Street for one in Hyde Street, which is a logical continuation, though not generally served by buses, of Jewry Street, so that every lunch time she passed by 'my' shop door. She sometimes even came into the shop – it was primarily a greengrocery though dabbling, and more to my interest, in home-made wine kits – to buy a derelict lettuce for her pet rabbit. By this time she had cut her lovely long hair short, firstly into Medusa curls and then into what is known, equally stupidly either way, as page-boy or bob. She still appeared utterly alluring - even though or perhaps because she was now far from the featherweight slip of a teenager she had been in the Southgate Street and Lodekka era - especially in multi-strapped but otherwise minimal if very high-heeled shoes and a flamenco style dress, and I think she knew how I felt about her, even in the brief moments of purchasing rotting lettuces, but she never gave me the slightest

encouragement, and I can only repeat the question I asked of Mary earlier in these lines, where are you now, the angel of then with VRs screaming past – with that odd but typical VR screech - beyond that up-turned nose and those strange grey eyes and that stinking lettuce.

Winchester was allocated four VRs. Or at least I believe they were allocated to Winchester, and there may have been more than four, but the four of which I am thinking were notable for their numberplates, these being issued in Bournemouth – because Bournemouth was obviously always the centre of H&D operations - and these four numberplates were YEL 1T and on to YEL 4T, so that the first bus was known, among mentally defective people such as this author who study registration plates, as Yell it! and the last as Yell for tea! So charming were these numbers that, according to legend, the buses in question were subsequently issued with new numbers and their plates sold off into the re-registration trade.

A hefty threat to the supremacy of the VR on the 47 arrived in the early 1980s with the secondhand London Transport DMSs. This scene, without a word of a lie, depicts Hampshire Bus no.1921 (OJD 203R) on the 47, but in the author's usual style it is far more concerned with shoe-straps and shoulder straps, and half a bus is good enough to prove it was there, isn't it!

Rear seat

As for my devotion to (or obsession for) Prudence, this was sorted out by Margaret, see above on rear seat of Leyland National. And Margaret and I rode on DMSs sometimes too. These vehicles were renowned of course for being a metropolitan disaster – well, I mean to say, it was obvious from the start, wasn't it, you can't have a London transport policy without an open-platform RM and a conductor on the back step any more than you can have it (as it appears) without a Red Ken – but, in thinly disguised form with the central entrance removed yet still plainly recognisable for what they had formerly been, they seemed to serve far less disastrously for H&D, and put in a lot of good work on the 47. There were ten of them, the lowest original fleet number being 2039 and the highest 2245, all registered either OUC-R or OJD-R, and with Hampshire Bus they received fleet numbers – randomly – between 1917 and 1926 and a red livery , latterly with the addition of blue and white stripes along below the lower-deck windows swept up diagonally at the rear.

Here I must allow myself a digression, not least because digressions are expected of me in my writings on omnibuses, and in this present work I have digressed so far only in the cases of Mary, Margaret and Prudence, and possibly postal, but furthermore because this next digression is actually a digression on the subject of buses, though not indeed on H&D buses. The subject is that at about this date Winchester was enjoying not only the secondhand London Transport DMSs but also an influx of secondhand London Transport Red Arrows, otherwise known as Merlins and/or Swifts. These came in from the wild east of Winchester, places such as Bishop's Waltham which probably don't really exist at all except in the mind of Providence and the Ordnance Survey, and belonged to a firm known as Hants & Sussex, a title provocatively imitative of Hants & Dorset and covering a far more chequered and diverse history. I would not dream of going so far as to use the word piratical, even in its omnibus connotations, though I have heard such an adjective quoted in relation to the firm in question. Be all this as it may, these elderly Red Arrows – vehicles not devoid of character even if unsuitable for the purpose for which they were conceived - certainly added a piquant touch to the Winchester bus scene. The vehicles most prominent upon it had registration numbers from the AML-H batch, though others were involved; thus even the youngest were much more antique than the Hampshire Bus exiles. Whether or not they were more suitable for this new

The early days of VR operation on H&D were somewhat clouded by the question as to whether they were to be one-man or one-person operated – the question here being the number of crew employed rather than a sexist issue – for with the FLFs it was always, obviously, a two-human-being job, and I must say that I had friends who were conductors who could entertain no idea of becoming a driver. One of these was an American. A Vietnam War drop-out who like many others of that generation had engaged in digging up the archaeology of Winchester as a convenient form of draft-dodging. With the demise of H&D conductors he worked for a while in the same Jewry Street greengrocery as me and then became a postman, and now, two decades later, is still a postman and one of the best-informed upon all the questions of postal delivery in Winchester

If the question of change from FLF to VR was fraught with such difficulties as these, the VRs anyway found themselves discomfited though not entirely ousted very soon afterwards – even if now well established as OMO – before a most unlikely rival, in the form of a London Transport reject, namely the DMS.

scene is uncertain, all I know is that in the last days of 1987 they disappeared, just like several famous Caribbean heroes from the bold tales of the High Seas faded away.

The greatest 47 variety – the bendibus. This appears to be the Winchester bendibus that very soon became a source of spare parts. It is about to follow those cars and then turn sharp left, testing its bendy qualities to the limit.

Bends

From this digression we must pass on to what must surely be the most serious digression of omnibus operation on route 47. It is essential at this point to state that Winchester was originally a Roman city, quite apart from any civilisation it enjoyed before the great days of the Roman Empire, and thus it had a street plan of rectilinear nature. This pattern, despite time and the more recent efforts of town-planners, has left its mark on the map, so that any bus entering or leaving Winchester must indulge in a series of right-angle bends. Especially on the 47. It has to be added that, at this stage in the proceedings, H&D had, since 1986, been operated by a Scottish chap called Stagecoach, and it was from somewhere up in Scotland that this brave fellow had picked up a couple of potential bargains from a firm known as McGills of Barrhead. These items had first seen light of day in the well-known Yorkshire city of Sheffield – famed for cutlery – and further famed as the first place in England to operate articulated buses, otherwise known as 'bendibuses', though for goodness' sake they had been familiar enough in sensible places such as Switzerland and Germany for many years or even decades before this date. These two bendibuses – or at least one of them – represented the new entry for Stagecoach's occupation of the streets of Winchester. Whether or not they were suitable for the streets of Sheffield – deprived of mass-moving trams since 1959

and allowed to have trams back again 30 years later – they were hardly suitable for the narrow and right-angle bends of Winchester. Nevertheless here they were. They looked something like Leyland Nationals, equipped with a continental tail. Though both of them may have operated for a very brief period one of them very soon retired simply to sit at the back of the Winchester bus station having more and more pieces taken off it to keep the other going. The other flung its tail about in Loch Ness fashion as it tackled the right-angles. In these circumstances the hinder portion provided a pretty exciting ride, but the rear doors never worked, even with pillaging from dead sister, so you always had to traipse up to the middle if not the front entrance to get out. The monster was plainly beyond the comprehension of the average 47 driver.

Nor did the surviving monster survive very long. No more than a matter of months, if I recall correctly. Perhaps the supply of vital organs dried up. Then, apart from the continued presence of VRs that probably outlived the DMSs, modernity caught up, in the shape of Stagecoach-liveried Alexander-bodied Leyland Olympians.

These were to be my last sight of the 47 because, finding the streets of Winchester ever more burdened with lager-louts, yuppies, and designer card shops, quite apart from what my opinion might be of a

Modernity comes to the 47 in 1989 in the form of a Stagecoach Alexander-bodied Leyland Olympian, but Jowitt plainly wasn't concentrating on it very hard.

Southampton Atlanteans. This scarlet interlude lasted some two or three years. Southampton Corporation Transport, by this time known in modernistic terms as City-Bus (with a pack of second-hand Routemasters to add verisimilitude to the title) found that interurban or rural activities such as the 47 involved biting off more than they could chew. Thus the 47 fell to Solent Blue-Line.

Solent Blue-Line is famous as the Isle of Wight's (or Southern Vectis') post-deregulation invasion of the mainland, a resounding success which spread blue-and-yellow buses (the yellow presumably representing the rare patches of golden sand to be found on the otherwise muddy Solent shores) over large tracts of the hinterlands of these shores. As Solent Blue-Line shipped quite a few ex Southern Vectis VRs – with the renowned Isle of Wight DL-series numberplates – to serve mainland routes it is a possibility that some of these may have served a turn now and then on the 47, a suggestion presumably permissible enough to risk in the pages of *Classic Bus Yearbook*. The last of these VRs are probably in their death throes as I write these words. So far as I know (writing now on the Isle of Wight to which I lately retreated when after ten years the escape from Winchester proved too cold and too isolated and too far from the sea, and even though the information may not really be merited in said pages) the fact is that the 47 still flourishes, with more modern types identical to the Southern Vectis buses I see every day except for being blue and yellow.

Perhaps I should brave a crossing on one of the most expensive (pro rata) ferry crossings in the world, and seek out a 47, and ride through to Winchester. Try to see, in the upturned twisted motorway landscape below what was once Mary's house, the approximation of where the old main road lay and where no.1145 must have travelled. Try to remember, though few or even none are now the same, the names of the shops in Southgate Street and Jewry Street past which my pretty Prudence tripped in her preposterous high heels. Try above all, even in a world where the delights of the back seat of a Leyland National are as dead and gone as the glory of riding on the open-rear platform of a 1930s Parisian Renault in the late 1960s, to hope that the magic and promise of those Margaret moments is not quite forever lost. **CB**

Leyland Olympian, I fled to a rural refuge some 130 miles distant. Had I but known it the Olympians were about to be turfed out . . .

Hearsay

I can relate what happened next only by hearsay, either because it happened after I had already left or, if it was when I was still there, my mind was elsewhere. Furthermore, such modern times would hardly merit a space under the title Classic Bus, were it not that in a peculiar situation some mildly classic buses were involved. So far as I understand it – under Stagecoach, Hampshire Bus, then entered into some exchanges of routes with Southampton Corporation consequent upon which the 47 was operated with the well-known red and cream

No4: Ribble Motor Services

CHECK POINT

Born: Preston, June 1919

Step-parents: British Automobile Traction which already had a branch in Preston, but bought into Ribble in 1920 and transferred its buses into the new business which then was expanded across north-west England. In 1927, BAT's Lancashire & Westmoreland Motor Services went into Ribble and four years later it bought Carlisle & District Transport from Balfour Beatty. By then, there had been another change of ownership.

Who was that? Tilling & BAT, formed in May 1928 to bring together most BAT and Tilling subsidiaries and which later gave the main line railways a share in its bus businesses. That arrangement lasted as long as Tilling & BAT, with ownership reverting to the BET group in 1942. It came into state ownership in 1968 when BET sold its British bus operations to the Transport Holding Company.

The most consistent features of Ribble? Its dark red and cream livery and its fondness for locally-built Leylands.

It always ran Leylands? No. The fleet was highly mixed until 1922, with Vulcans and a pre-World War 1 de Dion run alongside more familiar AECs, Daimlers and Karriers. Then it invested in large numbers of Leylands which came in such quantities that Ribble could boast an average age of just two years and nine-and-a-half months at the outbreak of hostilities in 1939. management at Frenchwood Avenue must have been reading the diplomatic signs and anticipating the worst when supplies were turned off.

It surely couldn't buy Leylands after 1942: Indeed not, and standardisation took a back seat to the tune of 12 utility Daimlers and 46 Guy Arabs. From the delivery of Burlingham-bodied PD1s in November 1946 until it began taking Bristols in 1968 (REs followed by VRs), it hardly bought anything else.

Hardly? The only exceptions were two batches of Sentinel underfloors – six with four-cylinder engines and Beadle bodies in 1949 and 14 all-Sentinel examples with six-cylinder engines in 1951. It's thought that these were bought as much to scare Leyland into supplying its Olympic and Royal Tiger (of which Ribble bought over 300) than with any real intention of buying this far-from-mainstream manufacturer's products in any quantity.

But it did depart from mainstream Leylands? Apart from buying large numbers of the sorts of double- and single-deck Leylands you would expect the largest operator in the region to order, there were some unusual batches. Like the 50 White Ladies, a type comprising 30 Burlingham-bodied PD1/3s delivered in 1949 and 20 East Lancs-bodied PD2/3s which came the following year. All were 8ft wide coach-seated machines painted in the 'reversed' cream with red relief livery used for Ribble's coaches. They operated some of the busier limited stop services across urban Lancashire.

Methinks they were not the only White Ladies: Youthinks correctly. Ribble was an early customer for the rear-engined Atlantean (even if it did revert to front-engined buses for a while) and had 20 supplied in 1961 to coach specification so some of the earlier bearers of the name could be cascaded on to more local service work, blushing in newly-applied red bus livery. The Atlanteans had followed 37 earlier, more luxurious Atlantean coaches, the Gay Hostesses which operated for most of their lives on London services and which were eventually replaced by less satisfactory Bristol VRLs.

Ribble's most distinctive features? Its CK and RN Preston registrations, its hexagonal fleetnumber characters and – on most double-deckers – its narrow, triangular destination boxes.

Alan Millar

RIBBLE

AMBLESIDE
BIRMINGHAM
BRIGHTON
BRISTOL
BLACKPOOL
BOURNEMOUTH
CARDIFF
CARLISLE
CHELTENHAM
COVENTRY
DERBY
DOVER
EASTBOURNE
EDINBURGH
GLASGOW
HARROGATE
ILFRACOMBE
KESWICK
LEEDS
LLANDUDNO
LIVERPOOL
LONDON
MANCHESTER
MORECAMBE
NEWCASTLE
NOTTINGHAM
PENZANCE
RAMSGATE
SCARBOROUGH
SOUTHPORT
TORQUAY

At Blackpool's Coliseum Bus Station in 1955, embarrassed looking senior Ribble managers display the destination blind from one of the company's express coaches – a Leyland, of course.

MAENCLOCHOG
– AN ELEGY?

**Maenclochog? Yes, says TONY MOYES, I remember Maenclochog.
Not the kind of place you'd visit on purpose, perhaps;
a place you'd come upon by accident . . .**

Lewis & Jenkins' Bedford OB JXW 872 with Duple Almet (all-metal) body pulls away from Crymmych on an afternoon return journey to Maenclochog. Crymmych School is visible in the left distance. All photos by Tony Moyes

I F YOU LIVED in Aberystwyth, and decided to have a short break in Tenby, then I suppose you could, as I did, find yourself driving home out of Haverfordwest on a late April afternoon in 1972. For a change I'd chosen the B4329 road which cuts directly across the Preseli hills to Cardigan, cutting off a corner and, I supposed, a few minutes. After ten miles or so, the farming country was getting less

Reversing out of Lewis & Jenkins' depot at Maenclochog in 1974, one of two standard Duple-bodied Bedford OB buses prepares for a school contract to Crymmych.

verdant and gentle, and we were beginning to climb. The signposts pointed towards curious names like Woodstock Slop, Castlebythe, Henry's Moat: a distinct frontier feeling. I remembered that there had been a thin bus service in this direction from Haverfordwest: a Western Welsh ex-Greens Motors offering which had been wiped out with others in late 1970. Tufton disappeared behind us; another non-place. Imagine my astonishment when, alternately ambling and bowling along ahead of us we came upon what appeared to be a Bedford OWB: white roof, the rest in fairly dark green. The flowing script on its rear left no doubt as to who this apparition belonged to O J Edwards and Sons, Maenclochog – phone Maenclochog 215. Funny, its registration number was a London one: JXX 461. Inside could be seen a passenger or two, their silhouettes more like those you'd expect 50 miles or so to the east in flat-cap-and-muffler industrial south Wales, rather than here, in rural Pembrokeshire. The next signpost pointed right, to Maenclochog, but the Bedford sped on. Thinking I'd be able to cut ahead of it, we turned right. After a couple of contorted miles

through two farmyards we hit the B4313, and in another mile were confronted by Maenclochog.

Fearsome

The road widened, splitting around a sort of village green; an unfenced large field flanked with a miscellany of buildings; poles and wires abounded. To the left was a primary school, cottages, tin sheds, an agricultural co-op, and the fearsome Hen Capel, a chapel undeservedly proud of its being re-fronted in 1904. Ahead, the backs of two buses pointed towards us; white roofs, pale green pillars and waistband, darker green below, and that same flowing script lettering as just seen. The left-hand vehicle was a cheerful enough wee Bedford J2 (894 UPP). The other was a Duple MkII bus-bodied Bedford OB, KGH 482), with rear and front not unlike the classic Duple Vista coach but with a straight waistrail and a good bold

O J Edwards' Central Garage, Maenclochog, with a bevy of Bedford OBs on show, August 1972.

destination box atop the front containing the magic word 'Maenclochog'. As a backcloth was a low stone church in a circular walled churchyard ringed with pine trees through which a drizzly wind was tugging.

And to the right? The post office, some more houses, one a stolid one that had probably been a farmhouse not long ago. There was hard standing alongside and a pair of corrugated sheds, the ensemble seemingly crammed with little Bedfords – at least six of them. There was one standard Vista coach, to be sure, but the rest were either straight waistrail, Duple bus-bodied, or what appeared to be OWBs, variously registered JXH or JXW, some of these latter in pale green. This was, as the Passenger Transport Year Book later revealed, the Central Garage, Maenclochog. Attention was now diverted by the unmistakable sound of an approaching Bedford OB: JXX 461 wheeling on to the forecourt. Eagerly I approached the driver. Yes, he'd come from Trecwn . . . perhaps the best place to see the OBs at work would be at Crymmych at school time . . . but he was expected home for tea. The journey on to Aberystwyth in the gathering gloom over the rounded crest of the Preselis was spent in mixed excitement and contemplation. This must surely be the biggest fleet of Bedford OBs around by the early 1970s, yet they weren't exactly well-known. What on earth were they up to?

As can happen, other things somehow got in the way of finding out more, for a while. But about 18 months later, disconnected events and findings rekindled the flame. Innocently skimming through some volumes of Commercial Motor for 1949 in the National Library of Wales, I came across a full-page advertisement for the Duple Almet body – clearly the angular type seen on O J Edwards' 'OWBs'. The one illustrated was described as meeting with approval from a sugar plantation owner on Barbados, its all-metal structure being less inclined to rot in the tropics. So that was it; the 'utilities' at Maenclochog were OBs, and it transpired dated from 1950. The clincher was a report in a PSV Circle newsletter that with effect from September 1973 Edwards' business had passed to E J Lewis and T L Jenkins, along with a fleet of 12 vehicles, seven of them OBs. These things had to be seen, and quickly. Surely the OBs couldn't last. As for Trecwn, incidentally, this I discovered was a military store carved into a valleyside near Fishguard at the outbreak of World War 2. By the 1970s it still employed about 600 people; from all over north Pembrokeshire they came and went each day by lots of psvs, to work in a troglodyte world.

Pilgrimage

According to my notes of a pilgrimage on 23 October 1973, I must have hared by car down the coast to Cardigan, pottered around the Moylgrove area looking for the then headquarters of the expanding independent Richards Bros, and duly finding its depot in a most improbable spot. There were the two vehicles taken over with the business of Williams, St Dogmaels, still in use (including ex-Western Welsh Albion Nimbus WKG 30), though the ex-Southdown Leyland PD2/12 OCD 771 was derelict. Across country, then, via Eglwyswrw and on to the northern flanks of the Preselis, I got to Crymmych.

If there is a gulch feeling about Maenclochog, Crymmych has much the same, though – or maybe because – an 'A' road runs through it. Overlooking the village – hardly a town – like some airfield control tower looms the main block of the secondary school, Ysgol y Preseli – a landmark for miles across this thinly but evenly-populated country. As if tethered around its flanks awaiting the finish of school were skeins of buses. some of which had been parked up all day. My eye was caught first by ex-Thames Valley Bristol LL6B FMO 938 in Jones, Login's turquoise and cream, on its own. But leading a rake of vehicles at a kind of island platform facing towards Cardigan was an 'OWB' displaying Maenclochog on its blind (JXW 872), now carrying the legal lettering of Lewis & Jenkins t/a Eltys Motors. Maenclochog. Behind was a Bedford SBG/Mulliner bus NGY 812, also obviously ex-Edwards, and a motley mixture of Ford 570E and Bedford SB coaches. Mostly they were from the Crymmych-based operators D J Jones and Rees

(Midway), and Duple-bodied, but there was one SB of Richards, Moylgrove, registered OLD 94, Harrington-bodied and new to Grey-Green. Rounding things off was a rare Bedford VAL with Weymann Topaz body, Jones of Login's JNK 686C.

A bell sounded. Children were now piling into this assortment; they clearly knew which was which. And yet, no Maenclochog drivers were to be seen. But wait; from afar the call of an OB getting closer. From a side road, there came another 'utility', JXX 487, with a handful of children and two extra drivers aboard. It joined the end of the line, the incoming drivers woke their steeds, and within what appeared to be seconds the Login and Maenclochog contingents had performed a deft U-turn in the main road and swept away south. I could just discern that the LL6B had headed straight down the Tenby road, whereas the Eltys vehicles had turned off the first side road, labelled for Mynachlogddu and Maenclochog; within half a mile this road had split into vague lanes, and each subsequent branch became more confusing. Of the OBs there was no sign; I'd have to come this way again!

Another visit

Six months elapsed before I could snatch another visit: 13 April, 1974. Again I took in the area west of Cardigan first, to record the Cardigan-Fishguard

Crymmych School departures, October 1974. Leading is Lewis & Jenkins' Bedford OB, KGH 481, followed by its SB, NGY 815, and OB, JXW 872.

service still being run by Roberts' Pioneer Motors of Newport at that time. Somehow I found myself approaching Maenclochog from the Fishguard direction. Not far from Greenway (a place, not a rebuilt National), where the course of the long-lost railway from Clunderwen to Letterston swung over the road, there was a bungalow whose garden was growing a crop of junked green vehicles of unmistakable Edwards origin. There was a genuine Bedford OWB, albeit re-registered (248 FDE); a standard OB coach, and, nearest, a short wheelbase Bedford ML van with windows but without evident registration plates. This was indeed the Edwards family house; yes, there would be some OBs at Maenclochog at 3.15pm or so; they took children back home to various villages that had lost their primary schools. One did carry on beyond Mynachlogddu to Crymmych with the extra drivers. And yes, you could well find an OB at Whitland Grammar School. Well, the Trecwn one would be taken home by its driver to Rosebush when it got back at 5.15pm or so. Take care, though; it ran earlier on a Friday. The picture was getting clearer.

Above: *Duple Almet-bodied Bedford OB JXX 487 waits on the verge outside Maenclochog Primary School in April 1974, carrying a destination – Hartwell – more appropriate to its earlier life at a Ministry of Defence establishment near Aylesbury.*

Opposite right: *A long way from Wendover, but Bedford OB/Duple Almet JXX 487 was quite at home in the bleak Preselis in July 1975 on a Crymmych-Maenclochog school run with Lewis & Jenkins.*

Down at Maenclochog, Duple composite-bodied OB, KGH 481, was backed out of the depot and driven round the green ready to do the Llanycefn contract. JXX 487 was waiting by the school to perform the Mynachlogddu-Crymmych run. Its destination box contained a blind full of place names around Aylesbury; The 'OWBs', I was now told, had been at a Ministry of Defence establishment near Aylesbury when new. By tailing JXX (but not being able to overtake, I didn't get photographs en route) I did establish where the route went, and was at last able to get some of the shots I wanted, of the Bedfords, and the LL6B, leaving Crymmych.

Opposite left: *Making for home – Eltys Motors Bedford OB/Almet JXX 461 potters along a lane near Rosebush on a Crymmych-Maenclochog school run in July 1978.*

Above: *Bedford Almet JXX 461 heads out for Crymmych past the Agricultural Co-op in Maenclochog in July 1975.*

Now the code had been cracked, it was very tempting to pop down from Aberystwyth occasionally to keep an eye on the OBs; sometimes one trip a year , sometimes less. By July 1974, the little Bedford J2 had appeared in a very tasteful steely blue and white livery, and so had 'OWB' JXX 487. This time, wittily, its blind was displaying 'Wendover'. Some of the spots that I thought would have been photogenic turned out not to be so, so there was always a reason to come back again.

Cute and snouty

However. on the way back from Tenby in March 1977, during the school holidays, the Central Garage contained some novelties not previously seen. There was quite a cute pale green snouty little Strachans-bodied Bedford J4 (XUC 548), ex-Edwards. But also, both neat in the new livery, were likewise Strachans-bodied Bedford VAS bus (KHU 455E) new to the Southmead General Hospital, Bristol, and an ex-Crosville Bristol MW coach (7622 FM). Almet-bodied OB JXX 461 was also found at its driver's home at the one-time slate-quarrying village of Rosebush looking good in blue and now sporting a blind which could well have come from one of the KGHs. But there appeared no sign of the latter, enough to

raise suspicion that time was running out for the OBs. What proved to be my last sighting of one at work was to be in July 1978 when I witnessed JXX 461 and the VAS/Strachans bus near the remote Ffeidr Wilym farm, where two quite separate contract routes momentarily joined. On that occasion too, I discovered that the Lewis business had relocated itself on the old railway station yard at Maenclochog, where in an incipient graveyard, engineless OBs were beginning to accumulate, and even the ten years younger XUC 548 sat dormant. Passing through Crymmych in June 1980 – it just happened to be at about 3.40pm – revealed no OBs, and literally and metaphorically I drew a line under what had been a marvellous episode.

And yet . . . in April 1993 the PSV Circle issued its admirable revised fleetlists of small operators in Wales. Idly flicking through, I came to the Lewis, Maenclochog entry. Lo and behold, three OBs (all Almets) were still recorded, but no longer registered. So one dusky late afternoon in December 1993, returning from a commitment in Haverfordwest, I called in at the Old Station Yard, and (with Mr Lewis's agreement) I pushed back the brambles and the saplings to try to diagnose what mossy bits of OB were which. JXW 858, JXX 461 and 487, yes. And here's KHU and XUC . . . As I paused, half pleased, half sad, a school bus splashed across the yard, coming off duty a Leyland Swift, or Cub, perhaps Wadham Stringer bus-bodied LUL 503X, ex-London Borough of Wandsworth. Could that look quite good, photographed against a background of the Preselis? Well here we go again . . ! **CB**

SUMMER WINE

JOHN S HINCHLIFFE looks back at bus services in Yorkshire's Holme Valley, better known to many as the setting for the long-running 'Last of the Summer Wine' television series

HOLMFIRTH, a small town set in a Pennine valley in West Yorkshire is the setting for the BBC's 'Last of the Summer Wine', which in 1997 celebrated 25 years as the longest-running comedy programme. The TV series has helped to promote Holmfirth as a tourist centre, and many of the visitors come by coach. When I spent my youth in the Holme Valley in the 1960s Holmfirth was a quiet town – shops even closed from dinner time on Saturdays; now many are not only open all day Saturdays but Sundays too.

In the 1960s Holmfirth was served by seven bus and coach operators, five of which ran stage carriage services. Huddersfield Joint Omnibus Committee ran various services from Huddersfield. These were: 35 and 36 via New Mitt and Scholes, continuing to (35) Marsden Hard End, (36) Slaithwaite; 37 and 38 via Honley and (37) Spring Villa, (38) Oldfield with 37 continuing to Parkhead; 47 and 48 direct continuing to Holmbridge and 48 to Holme, with contract services to Washpit Mills and

Above: *Huddersfield JOC 1950 AEC Regent III no.169 (EVH 569) with 56-seat East Lancs body at Holmfirth bus station on one of the additional journeys run on the Scholes service on Saturdays.*

Left: *With a Daimler CVG6LX behind, Huddersfield JOC no.200 (UVH 200), a 1962 AEC Regent V with 70-seat forward entrance Roe body at Holmfirth bus station.*

IN THE 1960s

school services to Holmfirth Secondary Modern School, and an annual service to Harden Moss, for the sheepdog trials. It was during the 1960s that Huddersfield Corporation coordinated its former Lockwood to Brackenhall trolleybus service with some of the JOC Holme valley services, routes 37 to 12, 38 to 14, 47 to 11 and 48 to 10 and extended to Brackenhall a large estate on the other side of Huddersfield.

Daimlers

Buses normally used by the corporation were Daimler CVG6s with East Lancashire or Neepsend bodies of batches 435-40 and 457-72, later being joined by Roe-bodied Daimler Fleetlines 473-503. Buses 472/3 are now preserved. The JOC normally provided its forward entrance buses of AEC, Daimler and Leyland manufacture as they had their destinations modified with a twin-track number blind for the service.

Routes 35 and 36 (Huddersfield) were mainly operated by single-deck buses and had been one-person operated since 1951 originally with buses of Guy manufacture, later AEC Reliances were used and the 1960s brought Leyland Leopards on the route until it was revised at the time of deregulation in

Top: *Photographed at Scarr End in 1951 running as a driver-only bus, Huddersfield JOC no.1 (FVH 1), a Guy Arab UF with 43-seat Guy body. It was still running peak extras on the Huddersfield-Scholes-Slaithwaite service in the early 1960s.*

Below: *A Yorkshire traction Dennis Lancet with Roe bodywork, no.848 (CHE 340), about to leave Huddersfield for Holmfirth.*

1986. The newest buses were usually allocated to this route until the arrival of the rear-engined bus as these were unsuitable for route 36 at Slaithwaite; some peak journeys used crew-operated double deckers, but rear platforms hit the road at Slaithwaite

The next main operator was Yorkshire Traction with routes 38 to Barnsley via Kexbrough and 86 and 86A to Huddersfield via Kirkburton. Yorkshire Traction also ran two express services on Saturdays X19 Barnsley to Manchester, and a summer service from Doncaster to Rhyl. Service 38 departed at 15 minutes past the odd hour – to confuse the passengers, JOC's 38 had departed at 14min past.

Yorkshire Traction allocated any type of bus to route 38; it could be a Saro-bodied Tiger Cub or a lowbridge Atlantean or even a Burlingham-bodied coach with manual door, Route 38 was timed at 70 minutes from Barnsley to Holmfirth but had 95 minutes to return to Barnsley, It was possible with a double-deck rebodied Leyland Tiger to maintain time all the way from Holmfirth to Barnsley in first gear. Routes 86 and 86A were usually operated by Park Royal-bodied Leyland Tiger Cubs prior to one-person operation when the route became 86 only; two Leyland Leopards were allocated, having been downseated with the removal of the front seats from 53 seats to 45.

West Riding

The large independent operator, West Riding, provided a two-hourly service to Pontefract via Wakefield and Ackworth; normally buses on this route were Guy Arabs with C H Roe lowbridge bodies and platform doors, but Leyland-bodied Leyland Titans or a Guy Arab without doors appeared from time to time. For a few days Leyland Tiger 39-seaters appeared to see if they could cope with loadings, which resulted in an order for single-deck Daimler Roadliner

Above: *Arriving in Barnsley after its slow (1hr 35min) journey from Holmfirth, Yorkshire Traction no.713 (XHE 220), a 1962 Leyland PD3A/1 with 73-seat Northern Counties body.*

Right: *At one stage West Riding operated buses from its infamous fleet of Roe-bodied Guy Wulfrunians on the Holmfirth-Pontefract service. No.960 (WHL 960) of 1963 is about to duplicate Yorkshire Traction route 38, in spite of the route number shown.*

Left: *West Riding not only operated Guy Wulfrunians, it also bought Daimler Roadliners. Plaxton Derwent-bodied no.133 (FHL 826D) is seen at Holmfirth on its first day in service in 1966.*

Below: *Leaving Holmfirth bus station on the X19 to Barnsley, North Western no.736 (LDB 736), a 1957 AEC Reliance with Weymann 43-seat body.*

buses, two of which were used driver-only on the 85 Holmfirth - Pontefract service. Their appearance actually increased patronage, with many journeys running full into Wakefield, but they proved to be unreliable as they failed to start when the engines were hot, resulting in engines being left running all day. The Cummings V6-200 engines were later replaced with Perkins V8 engines, which were slightly more reliable.

The final out-of-town operator to serve Holmfirth was North Western which ran a daily four-hourly service from Manchester to Barnsley, route X19; the normal allocation for this route were 30ft AEC Reliances, but regularly on the Friday evening service

two rear entrance Atkinsons or one 36ft AEC Reliance would be provided. This service was later combined with the X20 to run via Penistone and extended to Doncaster as X19 but all journeys were then operated by Yorkshire Traction.

Holmfirth had its own stage operator, Baddeley Bros, which ran a morning peak then an afternoon and evening hourly service to Penistone; Cubley via Dunford and/or Crow Edge with a additional Thursday morning bus for Penistone market; but ran hourly on Saturdays and two-hourly on Sundays with two regular drivers for afternoons and evenings and coach drivers filling in for other journeys,

Several interesting vehicles were used on the service to Penistone; on even-hour journeys Bedford SBs were normally used with either Duple coach or Mulliner bus bodies. All these had been purchased secondhand. The odd-hour journeys were provided by a Duple-bodied Bedford SB purchased new in 1954, an ex-County Motors Roe-bodied Leyland Tiger, an ex-Trimdon Motor Services Sentinel, a

Top: North Western no.834 (RDB 834), a 1961 AEC Reliance/Alexander 41-seater, at Holmfirth on the X19 service.

Above: An impressive line-up – the G W Castle fleet of the 1950s with Bedford, Commer and Leyland coaches; nearest the camera is a Harrington-bodied Leyland Tiger PS2. J. Morris Bray

Burlingham-bodied Bedford SBG (also purchased new in the mid-1950s), and an ex-Halifax Albion Nimbus. Almost every Monday to Friday journey ran a different route to suit local requirements, mainly the Hepworth Iron Co.

Coaches

Baddeleys also had a smart coach fleet that included two Leyland Royal Tigers with Burlingham Seagull bodies, and several Bedford SBs with Burlingham Seagull and Gannet bodies. With the closure of Burlingham, Duple bodies were then purchased including a Leyland Leopard with Alpine

Continental body for use on David Brown Tractors contracts provided for potential customers; this ran with a large DB sticker on the front screen. At weekends it normally ran to Bournemouth on hire to Yelloway. Bedford VALs with Duple or Plaxton bodies then became the normal purchases.

Top: *G W Castle's Ford Thames Trader 570E with Plaxton Consort bodywork, 5709 WX.*

Above: *Dating from the early 1950s, Bedford SB/Duple Vega EO 9689 from the Baddeley fleet in Holmfirth bus station.*

Above: *Sentinel STC6, OUP 578, from the Baddeley fleet.*

Left: *Seen on delivery from Plaxton in 1965, Panorama I-bodied Bedford VAL FYG 920C turns into Baddeley's Holowgate garage in Holmfirth.*

Holmfirth also had two other coach operators. G W Castle had a small mixed fleet of Leyland, Commer, Bedford and Ford coaches with bodies by Harrington, Plaxton, Duple and Yeates. Castle's later swapped its coach business with Baddeleys in return for taxis, although only one coach was involved, an ex-Hanson ex-Ivy Coaches petrol-engined Bedford with Plaxton body. Two Humber Pullman taxis had engines that had previously been in Commer buses. All Castle's other coaches were sold to a dealer, all having been purchased new.

The other operator was G B Hirst who started with minicoaches expanding with the former Castle's Bedford SB with Yeates Riviera body. G B Hirst soon had a modern coach fleet mainly of Ford manufacture, but also included a rare rear-engined Albion Viking with Park Royal body.

The only operators who still serve Holmfirth from the above are Arriva, which now run to Leeds via Wakefield, and Yorkshire Traction, which runs the former Baddeley's service to Penistone and a summer service to Crich from Huddersfield. **CB**

ROGER AND OUT

ROGER DAVIES looks back at buses from a busman's point-of-view

There are buses I remember . . .

BOOZE AND DRUGS and rock 'n' roll – there ain't none of these here. In the late 1960s in Sheffield Polytechnic, I had my own vice: buses. I was unashamed, blatantly marking up my photos in front of my flatmates. One day, one said to me: 'I envy you, having an interest.' Made me think.

It's about variety. A bus that on paper sounds the same could be totally different because operators had different tastes and specifications. Try comparing Weymann-bodied AEC Regent Vs from Sheffield and Rhondda from the mid-1950s and you will see what I mean.

I grew up in Cardiff. Then it boasted buses from five municipalities, six companies, had five bus garages for three different fleets and two head offices and works. At first, the bus to school was a huge trolleybus along the Cowbridge Road, sitting on the last place on the long seat over the back bogies

Some gorgeous Orions, Rhondda nos.412/6 in October 1969 at Porth depot. They are parked next to the bridge over the river that ran through the middle of the depot – I never came across that anywhere else. They are Weymann-bodied AEC Regent Vs. All photos by Roger Davies

This is a Weymann-bodied Regent too, Sheffield no.730, a Regent III only two years older than the Rhondda ones and drop-dead gorgeous. It's crossing Waingate on 30 October 1968; exactly one month later it ran a farewell tour as Sheffield's last exposed radiator bus.

looking out of the funny little window where the conductor used to sit in the flat fares days, listening to the motors and the wires singing. They were mostly steamed up and full and they were wall-to-wall . . . not just always one in sight, but three or four in sight. Then a move for the school and an endless variety of motorbuses on the 31, 32B or 50. Maybe a Regent V, a Leyland PD2, with East Lancs body (or occasionally with a gruesome MCW Orion one), a Daimler CVG6, a Guy Arab a Bristol KW6G or an AEC Regent III. The fabulous Regent IIIs (nos.1-20) always seemed to work the long and (for relatively flat Cardiff) hilly 50. They were great buses – so great they were too easy to drive to become trainers. They got scrapped instead.

All had the fleets had their own identities and were incredibly varied. Their drivers and engineers had to cope with hugely differing types. There were some common tastes. There was quite high support for exposed radiator Titans. Newport's Longwell Green-bodied ones were splendid and Merthyr's fleet of long East Lancs-bodied specimens were truly classic buses, particularly the later forward entrance ones. This was a sop to modernity, most fleets sticking to tried and tested rear entrance jobs except Newport who embraced Atlanteans, and ones with Alexander bodies at that. This was a bit outrageous,

but Cardiff's strange Alexander Arab Vs outdid them. Numerous low bridges dictated lowbridge double-decks, surely one of the UK's more appalling devices, and the fleets of Caerphilly, West Mon, Bedwas & Machen and Gelligaer could all turn out a decent helping of such things. Many had Massey bodies, horrible things made no more agreeable by the praise heaped upon them by other enthusiasts. Perched up on the front seat peering down to look out of the condensation-covered front window of a new West Mon one is a memory best forgot. Strangely, Pontypridd, Merthyr and Rhondda had no need for such things and maintained a fleet of highbridges despite being in the heart of South Wales. Looking back I have memories of depots full of buses. You could look down on Merthyr's at Nantygwineth Street and see lines of smart maroon buses apparently at any time. Pontypridd, or Pudka (the fleetname was P.U.D.C. in large gold letters) dark blue buses were in profusion in the depot whenever I visited. It was the massive requirement caused by shift changes at the pits that was responsible. The all-day requirement was small by comparison, a marked change to my days in the industry when you tried to eliminate peak-only buses as much as possible.

Pudka endeared itself to me by moving from Guys to a super fleet of little forward entrance Regent Vs, two with delightful Longwell Green bodies. Now here's a point: why did so many fleets go to little 65-seaters? People like Rhondda, South Wales and Western Welsh did it after building up large fleets of 70- and 77-seaters. They all needed conductors so the sums don't really add up.

And vehicle types fascinate. How was it that Merthyr needed huge double-decks whilst Aberdare, not a million miles away, was an early convert to the Grimsby Cleethorpes style of dual doorway Reliance? Some fleets were predominantly double-deck, others like Gelligaer mainly singles and some like Pudka a mind-blowing mixture. I'd love to know the decision-making process. I suspect driver-only operation had a hand in it, and this, coupled with the decline in the coal industry resulted in doubles being swept away. On top of all this was complicated joint working of routes . . . heady days!

Aberdare was fun. Classic ECW-bodied Bristol Ks and Ls still hurried around with wooden-slatted seats

Cardiff no.10 in April 1966 snow at Victoria Park. These 20 1950 AEC Regent IIIs were almost all different by then as a result of tinkering by the corporation. No.10 is just about an original East Lancs, but not nearly as nice as a Bruce-bodied version. Note the trolleybus overhead: the outer line is for terminating 8s, the inner for 10s not quite halfway on their lengthy trip to Ely.

Left: Same snow, same place, wall-to-wall huge number 8 trolleybuses across the road at my local terminus. They represent the three main types of double-deck Cardiff trolley. The front one, no.280, is a 1955 East Lancs single-door BUT 9641T; no.230 is a 1948 former dual-entrance East Lancs one and now preserved; no.262, just arriving, is a 1949 Bruce of Cardiff former dual-doorway specimen. Of course, the snow covers the differences . . .

– another pit influence – in a cream livery with maroon, almost purple stripes. You went through their depot at Gadlys to find yourself right in the middle of the Red & White depot. Just along the road was a Western Welsh one. NBC sensibly rationalised a lot of this, but, hey, it wasn't so much fun.

I well remember a non-stop run from Aberdare to Cardiff in a R&W Lydney-bodied Royal Tiger (DS5151 in R&Ws barmy fleetnumbering) a heady experience a bit like barreling along Nathan Road in a Kowloon three-axle Dennis Dragon with all the windows open. R&W was one of the few Tilling fleets around and in comparison with the exotica the BET companies fielded, it was, well, dull. An MW does not compare with a sleek Weymann Tiger Cub (of which Western Welsh had 180) and I well remember forcing myself to photograph some MWs as one day they would go. They did, so I'm glad I did. But I hear you cry, Lydney bodies . . . Lydney ! Well yes, but they were dull too and looked home-made, which in a way they were.

The BETs in contrast had all sorts of things. South Wales had a fleet that was like an extract from an AEC catalogue all turned out in businesslike dark red. They provided Swansea town services and I could only marvel at travelling into the town centre on a Renown. Western Welsh was a very early user of Atlanteans, a type so revolutionary it graced the pages of the revered Eagle comic on its release. The first 12 were sold to Hong Kong and I well remember

a sage old employee remarking 'goodness knows why, they boiled going to Barry Island'. WW got some gruesome MCW Orion PD2s as well but with front doors. I've never understood this. The bus I learned to drive on was an MCW Orion PD2 and a very pretty little thing it was too. Lots and lots of Orions were. It had an exposed radiator. Bung a Leyland tin front on them and the people at MCW seemed to suffer a spasm. Were they really narrower at the top? And why only Leyland tin fronts? Still, yet more variety.

And then there was the stunning brown and red Neath & Cardiff. This was classy stuff. I well remember the look of despondency on the face of a Western Welsh driver as we waved his common or garden Tiger Cub by to ride an N&C Reliance. It was snob value pure and simple, just like Pullman, and it was an error to throw it away. The staff loyalty was chucked out too; years later N&C staff still held a reunion dinner.

This was part of the NBC rationalisation in South Wales and much of it did make good sense. Geographically, Western Welsh became Eastern Welsh but that wasn't what it was all about. It was Western as in Great Western Railway, you see. Red & White joined it and with NBC livery its buses actually were red and white. A new name was thought to be a good idea (it never is) and a competition held. The winning 'Cambrian National', which even I could live with, was rejected as it didn't

Another classic, Merthyr Leyland PD3/4 no.109 of 1960 sits in Cardiff in March 1966. By then two batches of forward entrance ones were in service with a third due so this back-loader was a rarity. It was working the route between the two towns jointly operated with Rhondda and Cardiff. The corporations called it the 20, although Merthyr didn't do numbers whilst Rhondda called it 100.

easily translate into Welsh. So 'National Welsh' was invented. That wasn't popular in England, so the buses there reverted to Red & White. No, it's beyond me too. The effect on staff moral is serious but customers, who do notice such things, are also affected. We combined the excursion programmes with each company taking it in turns. Excursions are very personal things. Your 'Welsh Mountains and Porthcawl' is part of the very fabric of life. We began to get lots of complaints. It turned out that the R&W 'Welsh Mountains and Porthcawl' was different from the Western Welsh one. We upset a lot of people. That's variety you can do without.

When I went to Sheffield, I couldn't believe the local corporation buses provided all the city services and most of the out-of-town and long-distance ones as well. It was all to do with A, B and C fleets and the railways were mixed up in it again. To make up it was a superbly varied fleet. Regent Vs that looked like IIIs and vice-versa. Hordes of Fleetlines and Atlanteans

providing ordinary city services when, back in Cardiff, we had only just had our first ones. What's more, Leopards and PD2s with ECW bodies! I felt sorry for enthusiasts in places like Birmingham, photo a bus with a rear door, one with a front door and you were done, and London, an RT, RM and an RF, one each in green and red and that was it. Poor things.

So it's variety. Variety was less alluring when you were responsible for making the things go out and carry people.

NBC inched towards boring, but thankfully influxes of Park Royal AN68s, surely one of the most

Above: *Gelligaer kept a small fleet of double-deckers for its share of the mighty 150 service between Newport and Rhymney jointly run with Bedwas & Machen, Red & White and Western Welsh. At Trethomas in June 1969 is 1959 Longwell Green lowbridge Leyland PD2/40 no.23 in the red, white and green scheme favoured at the time, which also kept political sensibilities at bay. Gelligaer didn't do numbers either.*

Left: *An astounding mixture was Pontypridd – pronounced 'Pontypreeth'. No.78 is a 1957 rear entrance Roe-bodied Guy Arab LUF seen in Taff Street in June 1969, scene of the annual Taff Street Dash.*

handsome of buses and variously bodied dual-purpose vehicles kept variety alive. Maidstone & District had an incredibly varied fleet when I joined it in 1977. Depots had Reliances, Leopards, Panthers, Fleetlines and Atlanteans all over the place. My area engineer and I started to reallocate to cut down the variety at depots. This saved having to hold vast spares stock at each one and meant staff were more familiar with the reduced number of types.

One of the first jobs I inherited was converting a route to Leyland Nationals. It was a route that had big loads at peak but very little at other times. It linked Medway with Maidstone via nowhere in particular, but there are vast numbers of people who live in Medway and work in Maidstone and vice versa. I've often thought this daily dual-direction exodus sums up the lunacy of mankind. It was run

This is turning into a study of Longwell Green, but how can you resist the delightful Aberdare's Longwell Green 1958 Guy Arab IV no.58 in Main Street in August 1966.

using two Reliances at peak but the theoretical capacity of a National meant you only needed one bus. Sacrilege really and I can only plead the saving of a peak hour bus (see earlier) in my defence. Actually, it retained some interest in requiring later Nationals with different gearboxes as it climbed a very steep hill with a very sharp bend at the bottom. If the delegated Nationals (nos.3546/7) were not available and an older one had to be used, it often broke down – I recall no.3510 being a bit of a star at this trick. A number of head office staff used this bus

and were not slow to express their displeasure to me. Imagine my joy when at the head office Christmas lunch (as local area manager I was invited), I was placed next to one of the most vociferous complainants. I ordered extra wine and no.3510 soon faded from the conversation.

Maybe because of the variety or someone understanding that M&D was basically an urban operator, it was chosen for comparative trials of new bus types. Big groups can and still do as they have the capacity to fund such things. Social work really. Hence five Ailsas and five Metropolitans were pitted against two Gardner-engined VRTs and 2 Leyland-engined ones. After a brief holiday in Hastings, they were being reallocated to Medway to be used on heavy urban work over very difficult terrain. Cardiff's Regent IIIs would be in paradise. Honest, it's very hilly and is the largest urban area in the south-east outside London. Atlanteans were banned from the notorious Waterworks Hill, their fleetnumbers being prominently displayed in the inspectors office and tales of passengers having to walk up to join the bus at the top were still rife. The comparative buses were allocated to Luton depot, which was in Chatham and was the old tram shed. It's been knocked down now and replaced by houses called 'Tramways'. Bit silly really.

It made sense to put all the funny buses together so the fitters were used to a variety. If you put a small batch of oddities in a depot they inevitably were pushed aside if in trouble whilst people concentrated on what they knew. At Luton they knew just about everything; it worked well and drivers became used to driving all sorts of things. They were joined subsequently by five Metrobuses of three different types against five automatic VRs.

There should have been five Leyland Titans as well but they were so delayed that everyone realised they were a complex piece of Meccano designed for LT and they quietly faded away.

To replace them we were promised six Willowbrook Dennis Dominators. Buses out of the ordinary were of interest to drivers. At the time we were in the midst of negotiations over complete driver-only operation. Whereas we were in broad agreement, it was very delicate as about 100 jobs were involved. We met in a remote pub to talk it through and came to an embarrassed silence moodily moving our peas around the plate. The Union Man said 'Six Dennis Dominators would help'. It was tempting, but I knew what would happen if they broke so I offered him six new VRTs and he settled for eight. I was happy, I'd been allowed 10.

The Dominators, nos.5301-6, turned up sporadically. The first two, 5301/3, were 4in too high; there was much stroking of beards and the rest arrived only 2in too high. Don't ask me how. Into Luton they went and started a collection of Dominators. I can't comment on the booze and drugs and rock 'n' roll, but it kept variety alive in Chatham. **CB**